What people are saying about...

OUR COMMON PRAYER

"My three desert island books: The Bible, *The Brothers Karamazov*, and the Book of Common Prayer. But when I point people to the classic English prayer book, they aren't quite sure what to do with it. Winfield Bevins has done us a great service by providing a clear and concise guide to the Book of Common Prayer. I recommend *Our Common Prayer* to those who want to learn how to pray well."

> **Brian Zahnd**, Author of *Beauty Will Save the World*
> and lead pastor of Word of Life Church, St. Joseph, MO

"Winfield Bevins has given us a warm and inviting introduction to the Prayer Book worship tradition. It will be a valuable resource not only for those who are new to the Anglican way, but also for Anglicans who have not discovered the value of the Daily Office. Winfield's personal journey has enabled him to appreciate the common prayer tradition as "an oasis in the desert, a river in dry and thirsty land, and a treasure hidden among the clamor of our postmodern society." I hope that *Our Common Prayer* will help many others find this treasure, as well."

> **The Rt. Rev'd John Guernsey**, Bishop of the Diocese
> of the Mid-Atlantic

"Winfield once again opens up the wonders of our rich heritage to the modern worshipper. He encourages us to step out of our fast moving world of novelty and constant change and, for a short moment, join the simple daily rhythm and pattern of devotional life established by Thomas Cranmer over five centuries ago. The enduring message and intention being the same now as it was then: that each of us might grow in our love for God through a greater understanding of His love for us, the unworthy. A timely book for today's church."

Andy Piercy, Director of the School of Worship, Song Writer, and Record Producer

"A few years ago, I experienced a dryness in my prayer life. I had a list of requests, but no overall structure in which to present them. A good friend gave me *The Book of Common Prayer* as a help. Written prayers were new to me. I approached the written prayers of past saints much as a child trying on the shoes of his dad. Would my feet ever fit into the spiritual shoes of the giants who have gone before me? I decided to pray those prayers, to pray Scripture, to pray the psalms, and to let my prayer life be shaped by the beauty of the written word. Over time, I found even my spontaneous prayers were reinvigorated. Winfield Bevins wants to introduce the beauty and majesty of Cranmer's work to a new generation. My prayer is that you will find your soul enriched by the biblical truth expressed in these prayers, and that through the Spirit, your heart will grow in reflecting the Savior."

Trevin Wax, Managing Editor- The Gospel Project LifeWay Christian Resources, Nashville, TN

"There are a few books that need to be on the shelf of every active Anglican. The Bible, of course. A personal journal. A copy of the Book of Common Prayer. And now this book, "Our Common Prayer." The treasures of Anglicanism have always been within reach inside the Prayer Book, but many people have needed a guide book to the book. Now they have it. Count me among those who use this book... and give many copies away!"

The Rev. Canon David H. Roseberry, Christ Church, Plano, TX

"Having grown up within the Anglican Tradition I am quite familiar with the power and beauty of the Book of Common Prayer. Countless times I have found myself in personal and pastoral situations, both joyful and tragic, with the rhythms and vocabulary of ancient prayers on my lips. These words, these prayers drawn from the Scriptures themselves and prayed thousands of times have shaped and molded my heart, my will and my mind. In this field guide, Winfield Bevins wonderfully and helpfully re-introduces the well worn path of faith found in the Book of Common Prayer to a new generation of Christians. And in this offering we find not only a pastoral tool but also a method of discipleship itself. A discipleship rooted in Scripture, regularly prayed, shaping our desires, our will and our intellect."

The Rt. Rev'd Steve Wood, Bishop of the Diocese of the Carolinas and Rector of St. Andrew's Church, Mt. Pleasant, SC

"Winfield Bevins shows the contrast of the prayer book with postmodern culture. *Our Common Prayer* provides an anchor in the waves of postmodernity. The connection to the past gives a deeper sense of meaning to worship that today is tossed around by the latest church fads. I believe this is why Anglicanism is going to continue to grow because it is missional yet also connectional to the past. The prayer book is just one practical example of the richness of Anglicanism."

Page Brooks, Pastor of Canal Street Church and
Assistant Professor at New Orleans Baptist Theological
Seminary

"Winfield Bevins has provided a great resource for the body of Christ. *Our Common Prayer* is a helpful and timely field guide for all of us who are interested in using *The Book of Common Prayer*, but come from a tradition where prayer books are not commonly used. If you are looking for a way to draw deeper benefit from *The Book of Common Prayer* or you want to help others enter into this important prayer book, I highly recommend *Our Common Prayer*."

Dr. Derek Vreeland, Author, *Primal Creedo: Your
Entrance Into the Apostle's Creed*

OUR COMMON
PRAYER

A FIELD GUIDE TO THE BOOK OF COMMON PRAYER

BY WINFIELD BEVINS

Foreword by ASHLEY NULL

SIMEONPRESS.COM

Our Common Prayer: A Field Guide to the Book of Common Prayer
Published by Simeon Press

Cover Design: Josh Shank www.rocketrepublic.com

Printed in the United States of America

ISBN-13: 978-0615824666
ISBN-10: 0615824668
1. Book of Common Prayer 2. Prayer 3. Daily Office 4. Anglicanism

For Charles and Della

with love and gratitude

CONTENTS

ACKNOWLEDGMENTS

The great English poet John Donne once said, "No man is an Island." Likewise, no book is written in isolation. Every book, no matter how big or how small, is the result of various influences on an author's life. I would like to offer a special thanks to the following people who have played a part in writing this book.

To the men and women of Church of the Outer Banks for allowing me to be their pastor. To Billy Diggs and Kelly Macko for their love and support during this project. To Kyle Tribett, Griff Crews, and Crissie Weeks for their editorial assistance with this manuscript. To Brian and Charlene Cerza and Daniel Barlow for helping me with the title.

To Bishops Steve Wood and John Guernsey for helping me embrace the prayerbook tradition for myself. To Scott McLucas, Alan Hawkins, and Kris McDaniel for showing me the missional aspect of the prayerbook. To my friends Marty and Jennifer Reardon at Trinity Anglican Mission in Atlanta, as well as Andy and Judy Piercy of the School of Worship for playing a significant part in my spiritual journey through worship.

To the team at St. Andrew's Church in Mt. Pleasant, South Carolina for their encouragement and support. To Ashley Null, one of the world's leading Anglican scholars, for writing a wonderful foreword and offering an introduction to Cranmer's passion for prayer.

To Charles Gill for being an amazing example of what it means to be a pastor and encouraging me in so many ways. It is a great honor to serve with you in the ministry.

Last, but certainly not least, I would like to thank my amazing wife, Kay, and our beautiful daughters Elizabeth, Anna Belle, and Caroline for allowing their daddy to spend time on the computer to write this book.

FOREWORD

by Ashley Null

Thomas Cranmer, the father of English-language liturgies, believed that prayer changes lives and nations. For when individuals and communities open themselves up to God's healing love, they at last find rest for their souls. Cranmer was convinced that this gift of inner peace is so rare, so profound, so life-changingly satisfying, that even the ever-prone-to-wander human heart will, out of sheer gratitude, fall back in love with God. So prayer renews our desire to serve God and others and all because of a fresh realisation that God has loved us first.

Love. For Cranmer, love lies at the root of everything. What the heart loves, the will chooses and the mind justifies. Because of Adam and Eve's disobedience, human beings are born miswired. That means, on our own, our hearts are addicted to self love. We naturally then choose to put ourselves first. And when we begin to experience the negative consequences of our selfishness, we simply rationalize our behaviour as merely pursuing our right to be happy. Without God, we stick to this pattern come what may. Even when putting ourselves first hurts others and makes us end up lonely. Even when being alone is the last thing our ever-longing-for-love heart wants. All too often we are our own worst enemy. We always seem to be short-circuiting our attempts at finding lasting love and happiness.

What, then, is the way out of our cul-de-sac of selfishness?

We need a heart transplant! And that is just what God himself promised to give us. He says he will give us a new heart. He also says he will give us his Spirit to move our new hearts to keep to his ways (Ezekiel 36:26-27).

Here, of course, is where prayer comes in. We all know that the church community is a hospital for recovering addicts to selfishness. What we too easily forget is that prayer is the operating room where we open our hearts to God so he can keep pouring his Spirit into us to address the problem. Even though we received a new heart when Jesus came into our lives, we still need fresh, daily doses of the Holy Spirit to move the rest of our body and soul to follow its godly rhythm.

How does this operating room work?

It's very simple. Prayer is just meditating on God's promises to us in Scripture. We matter-of-factly present our current situations to him in the light of his Word. And then we ask him to conform our desires, actions and circumstances to his will. Now God's voice is just like the human voice. His breath goes forth with his spoken words.

So as we dwell on his purposes for us which are uniquely revealed in the Bible, his Spirit works the truth of those divinely proclaimed words deep into hearts. In face of the cross of Christ, we realize afresh how much God loves us. Despite all our shortcomings, neediness, and anxiety. Despite even our determined desire for self-reliance. God loves us unconditionally. As we cast our cares upon him because he cares for us, as we are, divine grace brings forth human gratitude. We find a renewed love for him arising from deep within us. With hearts now strengthened once again to love God more than selfishness, our wills choose to serve him and others, and our minds line up all our priorities accordingly.

Thomas Cranmer's famous opening prayer for Holy Communion aptly expresses this need for grace to grab our hearts so that gratefully love and service will follow:

> Almighty God, to whom all hearts are open, all desires known and from whom no secrets are hidden, cleanse the thoughts of our hearts by the inspiration of your Holy Spirit, that we may perfectly love you and worthily magnify your Name, through Jesus Christ our Lord. Amen.

As we persist in grateful prayer, God's love for us begins to get the last word. Gradually, our bodies and souls learn to listen to our new, God-given heart beat. More and more we discover how to lead our lives in rhythm with God's own heart. His love for us, as we are, slowly works to bring out in us a godly love which moves us to become more like the people we have always wished to be. In the end, God's unconditional love for us draws an unconditional love from us for him and others.

Constant prayer, then, is the key to the Christian life. Of course, that is the whole point of the Parable of the Persistent Widow (Luke 18:1-8). We do not pray to God day and night because he is an unjust judge that needs to be prompted. We pray to him day and night because we need to be prompted. We struggle so much with injustice— the wrongs that others do to us, and the wrongs that we do to others. We pray to God day and night so that his love might renew a right spirit in us. We pray to God day and night for him to work in us so we can forgive others their wrongs and give ourselves away in godly service. In short, we pray day and night, not to move the heart of God to want to do our will, but for God to continually move our hearts to want to do his will.

But how can we persist in prayer day and night? What do we say? How do we keep from repeating ourselves? How can we make sure we think about the needs of others just as much as we talk to God about our own problems? In the face of a thousand different things we must get done today, how can we make sure we don't forget to pray? Or worse, how we do prevent ourselves from just getting so busy that we simply decide we don't have time to pray daily and stop trying?

The church's answer is the common prayer tradition. Our generation is not the first one to wrestle with these very real, practical problems. All Christians through the ages have faced them. So centuries and centuries ago the church began to develop material to help people know what to say, what to read and when to read it. Already by 500 AD, it had become customary for some Christians to leave the world of every-day affairs to live together in special religious communities which were dedicated to the rhythm of saying prayer seven times a day.

In 1549, Thomas Cranmer took this ancient monastic tradition and devised something more practical for Christians still involved in work in the world. His genius was to insert regular times for prayer at two natural points in the rhythm of daily life—at the beginning of our work day and at its end. He also had the good sense to translate all the ancient prayers he used into English and to make sure that they clearly proclaimed the Gospel of grace and gratitude. Finally, Cranmer devised a system for reading through the Bible in a year as part of the rhythm of daily prayer. He thought it absolutely essential that Bible reading and prayer time went together. For Cranmer was convinced that the words of Scripture were the spigot of the Holy Spirit. That's why he used so many biblical phrases in the prayers he himself wrote. Many Christians who have used Cranmer's pattern of prayer would agree.

By opening their hearts twice a day to God, generations of believers have found the Holy Spirit working in them as a result.

Dr. Bevins is to be commended for making the riches of Cranmer's daily prayer cycle fresh, appealing and, most importantly of all, easily available to a new generation. Now, more than ever, we all need divine help to have our hearts beat together with God's and one another's.

Ashley Null,
Faculty of Divinity
Cambridge University
Shrove Tuesday, 2013

INTRODUCTION
The Great British Invention

"There are two books in the English language which stand out pre-eminent above all others, which are better known and greater even than the works of our greatest poets. They are the Bible and the Book of Common Prayer."
-Percy Dearmer

I love all things British. The United Kingdom has given the world many great things over the years: Shakespeare, tea, crumpets, the Beatles, and fish and chips, to name a few. 2012 was a big year for the British people, as London hosted the Olympic games and Queen Elizabeth celebrated her Diamond Jubilee. However, even more important than these, 2012 marked the 350th anniversary of the Book of Common Prayer. Author and theologian J. I. Packer reminds us of its influence, "Long before the age of fish and chips, the Book of Common Prayer was the great British invention, nurturing all sorts and conditions of Englishmen and holding the church together with remarkable effectiveness."

The Book of Common Prayer has been read by millions around the world and still influences Christians today; it is one of the most beautiful prayer books ever composed. It is an old devotional book meant to be used in private and public prayer. The Book of Common Prayer is the second most widely read English religious book next to the King James Bible. It contains orders of services, ancient creeds, communal prayers, and a lectionary, which is a suggested reading plan for use throughout the year.

A few years ago, I discovered the Book of Common Prayer, and a whole new world opened up to me. I grew up attending non-traditional churches that did not value church tradition. In fact, they were skeptical and suspicious of anything outside of their own church beliefs. I gleaned a lot of important things from my church background, such as being "born again" and being "Spirit-filled." However, there was always something missing, and I couldn't figure it out. My personal prayer life was missing a rhythm, routine, and order.

I had been trying to pray on my own, by myself, and in my own strength. The historic prayers from the Book of Common Prayer gave me a new sense of balance and stability that I had never known before. These prayers were scriptural and had substance, and although they were very old, their words were timeless and full of life and vitality. As I began to use the Book of Common Prayer in my personal and private devotions, I fell in love with the common prayer tradition.

The Book of Common Prayer helped me realize that I am not just an independent contemporary Christian tied to my own time. We are a part of the larger body of Christ. Author Robert Webber reminds us:

"Our family tree began, not with the Reformation or the twentieth-century evangelical movement, but with Jesus Christ. This rich tradition continues through the Apostles, the primitive Christian community, the Apostolic Fathers, the Eastern Orthodox Church, the Catholic Church, the Church of the Reformation, and all who say, "Jesus is Lord."

A unique feature of the Book of Common Prayer is that our faith is meant to be shared in "common." Common doesn't mean something that is ordinary; rather, it means something that is shared in common together with others. Common is the root of the word "community" and refers to something we do or share together. The Book of Common Prayer was originally designed to unite the people in worship through a common prayer where both the minister and the people prayed together. Former Archbishop of Canterbury George Carey said, "The fundamental purpose of celebrating common prayer is this: to help the Church as a whole to pray together daily in a reflective and structured way." This stands in contrast to our radically individualistic world.

The truth is, many contemporary people are longing for a faith that was not started yesterday and is not driven by fads or personalities. The Book of Common Prayer offers a refreshing alternative to our postmodern world by helping us reconnect to the historic Christian faith. By praying with the common prayer tradition, we find that we are never really praying alone. Whether we are alone in a room or gathered with others in a small group, our prayers are united with believers both past and present. This is what theologian Scot McKnight describes in *Praying with the Church*, where he distinguishes between praying in the church and with the church. Common prayer unites us with other believers around the world who are praying the same rhythm of prayer throughout the day. The Body of Christ has always been and always will be a praying church. Prayer is one of the things that unites us- we all pray.

The Man Behind the Tradition

The complex history behind the common prayer tradition centers around one man, Thomas Cranmer. Cranmer was the most influential religious leader of the English Reformation and was instrumental in producing the Book of Common Prayer. Cranmer was one of the most complex and paradoxical leaders in all of church history. His influence spanned the reigns of three monarchs: Henry VIII, Edward VI, and Mary I. He was a brilliant theologian and churchman who was a strong leader when he needed to rise to the occasion, but at times he was also weak and frail. In the end, his lasting contribution to the universal church came through a prayer book.

On March 30, 1533, Cranmer was appointed Archbishop of Canterbury which allowed him to use his new found religious influence to openly embrace and promote Reformation ideals throughout England. Thomas Cranmer carefully danced around the politics of his position, and was able to pass reforms within the Church of England. Cranmer sponsored the Great Bible in 1539, and under the reign of young Edward VI, Cranmer was allowed to make the doctrinal changes he thought necessary to the church.

Cranmer's greatest achievement was realized in 1549 when he helped organize the Book of Common Prayer. Crammer and a committee of twelve of "the most learned and discreet bishops, and other learned men" compiled the prayer book from various sources, including ancient prayers of the early church, Catholic and Orthodox liturgies, as well as private devotions of the Middle Ages. They translated many of these sources into the English language.

Before the Book of Common Prayer, the prayers and worship of the Church of England were in Latin, which the common person did not understand. The Book of Common Prayer changed all of that by giving English-speaking people everywhere prayers in their own language for the first time in history! Imagine if there were no prayers in your own language? The Book of Common Prayer helped shape the devotional language of the English people by giving them a simplified prayer book in their own language that they could use anywhere, whether at church or at home.

The influence of the Book of Common Prayer on English-speaking people cannot be overestimated. Over time, the Book of Common Prayer eventually influenced the development of the English language itself. According to historian Diarmaid MacCulloch, the Book of Common Prayer is, "one of a handful of texts to have decided the future of a world language."

Contemporary author Daniel Swift recently wrote about the essential influence of the Book of Common Prayer on the English people and their language in *Shakespeare's Common Prayers: The Book of Common Prayer and the Elizabethan Age*. Swift said, "The Book of Common Prayer is an extraordinary and too-often neglected work... it is a skeleton beneath the skin of the best-known literary works of our or any time."

The influence of Cranmer's Book of Common Prayer is still felt around the world today. The words of the Prayer Book have become a familiar part of the English language, and after the Bible, it is the most frequently cited book in the *Oxford Dictionary of Quotations*. Like the King James Bible and the works of Shakespeare, many words and phrases from the Book of Common Prayer have entered popular culture. It has given us popular phrases, like "ashes to ashes" and "till death do us part." Lutherans, Methodists, and Presbyterians alike have borrowed from the Book of Common Prayer, and the marriage and burial rites have found their way into those of other denominations and into the English language.

Not only is the Book of Common Prayer widely used throughout the English speaking world, but it also appears in many variations in churches in over fifty different countries and in over 150 different languages. The Anglican Church has grown to become a worldwide family of churches which has more than seventy million adherents in thirty eight provinces spreading across 161 countries. The Anglican Communion is the third largest body of Christians in the world and is one of the fastest growing in Asia and Africa. Located on every continent, Anglicans speak many languages and come from different races and cultures, and their love for the Book of Common Prayer is one of the things that holds them together.

Over 300 years ago, the great revivalist John Wesley once said, "I believe there is no Liturgy in the world, either in ancient or modern language, which breathes more of a solid, scriptural, rational piety than the Common Prayer of the Church of England." The Prayer Book is a literary masterpiece that continues to be a source of spiritual inspiration for millions around the world by bringing together a unique balance of doctrine and devotion in a majestic way.

Using this Book

Our Common Prayer is for contemporary readers who are interested in learning more about the common prayer tradition. Whether you come from a traditional or non-traditional church background, you will find this book a helpful aid to your prayer life. I believe that the historic common prayer tradition still has something to offer contemporary Christians, and I want to encourage a whole new generation of believers to discover it for themselves.

The purpose of a field guide is to help readers discover a new subject for themselves by immersing them in the "field" of the subject matter. *Our Common Prayer* is a field guide that offers an actual immersion into the life of prayer from beginning to end. It is not like a book that you read from start to finish; rather, you can start in any of the sections and go back and forth as you choose. In fact, you can use a portion from each section every time you pray.

Our Common Prayer follows a simple outline and rhythm from the Book of Common Prayer and is edited for contemporary use. *Our Common Prayer* can be used in a variety of ways: for individual private devotion, for small groups, for youth ministry, or even for church gatherings.

The first chapter offers a simplified form of the Daily Office containing morning and evening prayers that can be used by small groups or individuals. You can use the Daily Office at your own pace. As you follow the Daily Office, allow yourself to slowly get into the rhythm of praying it in the morning and evening.

The second chapter contains a variety of beautifully written prayers and thanksgivings that can be used for various occasions. You will find that this collection of prayers, both ancient and contemporary, will enrich and deepen your personal prayer life.

The third chapter contains several forms of intercessory prayers for the sake of others. These prayers will lead you to pray for several different areas of concern: the church, the nation, the world, the local community, and those who suffer or are in need.

The fourth chapter shows how our beliefs ultimately shape our prayer through affirming the historic Creeds of the Christian Church. The creeds offer us a concise summary of the essentials of the Christian faith that help form our spirituality and unite us as followers of Christ.

The fifth chapter contains a selection of prayers from various historic saints from the early to middle ages. These ancient prayers are timeless. They will inspire you to emulate the faith of great saints who have gone before and help you grow deeper in your walk with Christ.

The sixth chapter is a collection of prayers that follow the church calendar and can be prayed throughout the week or on Sunday morning. They can be prayed each week and will help you follow the church calendar in a more meaningful way.

The final chapter introduces the reader to an ancient Bible reading plan called a "lectionary." A lectionary is a systematic way of reading through the Scriptures throughout the year, either in private or public worship. The Lectionary readings from the Book of Common Prayer were originally intended to be used for morning and evening prayers.

My prayer is that you too will discover the rich, historic, spiritual tradition of common prayer for yourself. Come and see what millions of Christians around the world have come to know and love in the regular practice of common prayer. These prayers help us connect to the historic Christian faith. They remind us that we are not alone, but that we are a part of a larger Christian family that spans the pages of church history. May God bless you as you join with millions of others around the world who have discovered the common prayer tradition!

Merciful God, through the work of Thomas Cranmer you renewed the worship of your Church by restoring the language of the people, and through his death you revealed your power in human weakness: Grant that by your grace we may always worship you in spirit and in truth; through Jesus Christ, our only Mediator and Advocate, who lives and reigns with you and the Holy Spirit, one God, for ever and ever. Amen.

Chapter 1

PRAYING THE HOURS
Discovering the Daily Office

"None of us will ever find a better pattern for private prayer and Bible-reading anywhere than that offered by the Prayer Book's own daily offices." -J.I. Packer

We are creatures of habit. We all have rhythms, routines, and rituals that make up our daily lives. Most of us wake up in the morning and drink a cup of coffee, brush our teeth, and read the newspaper. Or maybe we start the day off with a simple prayer and Bible reading. Routines and rituals are not a bad thing. They keep us on track and remind us of what matters most. In a spiritual sense, I believe that we need to have rhythms and routines to grow in our daily walk with Christ.

The Book of Common Prayer contains what is commonly called the Daily Office or Divine Office, which is based on the ancient practice of prescribed daily times of prayer. The name comes from the Latin *officium divinum* meaning "divine office" or "divine duty." These services are accompanied by daily Scripture readings which include a reading from the Psalms, Old Testament, the New Testament, and a Gospel reading. The Daily Office includes prayers for morning, noon, and evening.

The Daily Office originated from the Jewish practice of daily prayer in the Old Testament. God commanded the Israelite priests to offer sacrifices of animals in the morning and evening (Exodus 29:38-39). As time went on, the Jewish people began to follow Torah readings, Psalms, and hymns at fixed hours of the day. By the time of the Roman Empire, forum bells began the work day at 6:00 in the morning, sounded mid-morning break at 9:00, the noon meal and siesta or break at 12:00, the recommencing of trade at 3:00, and the close of business at 6:00. Christians began to order their prayer life around these times of the day.

By the second and third centuries, early church fathers such as Clement of Alexandria, Tertullian, and Origen wrote of the practice of the Daily Office. The prayers were prayed both individually and in group settings, as in monasteries. Monasteries followed the fixed hours of prayer individually and corporately. As the monasteries continued to grow and spread throughout the Ancient Near East and into Europe, the monks took the practice with them.

The most influential monastic rule was established by St. Benedict of Nursia in the sixth century for the community of monks at Monte Cassino. St. Benedict established a "little rule for beginners" that brought together a balance of work and prayer. Pope Gregory the Great learned of Benedict's simple rule of prayer and adopted it for the larger Roman church. These hours of prayer continued through the Middle Ages and into the Reformation. Thomas Cranmer condensed the Daily Office into Morning and Evening Prayer, which many Christians still observe today.

Many people find that praying the Daily Office helps add a sense of regularity and balance to their prayer life. The Daily Office can help center you in the morning before you begin your busy day, and it can help calm you as you prepare for the hours of the night. Praying through the Daily Office is an enriching way that millions of Christians around the world practice daily devotions.

The Daily Office is a meaningful way to begin and end the day in prayer. Below is an abbreviated Daily Office with Morning and Evening Prayer. There is also a simple step-by-step outline to guide you. Remember, as you begin, don't rush. Reflect on the words and take your time. Mediate on what you're praying and saying to the Lord. Whenever you pray plural pronouns like "we" or "our," remember that you are joining your voice with other Christians who are also praying the Daily Office.

Morning Prayer

Opening Verses

Read one of the following sentences of Scriptures to prepare your heart for prayer.

Grace to you and peace from God our Father and from the Lord Jesus Christ. *Phillipians 1:2*

I was glad when they said to me, "Let us go to the house of the Lord." *Psalm 122:1*

Let the words of my mouth and the meditation of my heart be acceptable in your sight, O Lord, my strength and my redeemer. *Psalm 19:14*

Confession of Sin

Take a few moments to pray to confession your sins and acknowledge your need for God's grace and forgiveness.

Most merciful God,
we confess that we have sinned against you
in thought, word, and deed,
by what we have done,
and by what we have left undone.
We have not loved you with our whole heart;
we have not loved our neighbors as ourselves.
We are truly sorry and we humbly repent.
For the sake of your Son Jesus Christ,
have mercy on us and forgive us;
that we may delight in your will,
and walk in your ways,
to the glory of your Name. *Amen.*

End by acknowledging God's mercy and realizing that He has forgiven your sins in Christ Jesus.

May Almighty God have mercy on us, forgive us our sins, through Jesus Christ our Lord, and strengthen us to live in the power of the Holy Spirit, all our days. *Amen.*

The Invitatory

Move to a time of praise by praying the Invitatory and then the Gloria.

Lord, open our lips and our mouth shall proclaim your praise.

Glory to the Father, and to the Son, and to the Holy Spirit: as it was in the beginning, is now, and will be for ever. *Amen.*

The Psalm

Read the following Psalm or another one from the Psalter.

Come, let us sing to the Lord; let us shout for joy to the Rock of our salvation. Let us come before his presence with thanksgiving and raise a loud shout to him with psalms. For the Lord is a great God, and a great King above all gods. In his hand are the caverns of the earth, and the heights of the hills are his also. The sea is his, for he made it, and his hands have molded the dry land. Come, let us bow down, and bend the knee, and kneel before the Lord our Maker. For he is our God, and we are the people of his pasture and the sheep of his hand. Oh, that today you would hearken to his voice! *Psalm 95:1-7*

The Reading

At this time, you may read one or more additional readings from the Old Testament, New Testament, and the Gospels.

Blessed be the God and Father of our Lord Jesus Christ! By his great mercy we have been born anew to a living hope through the resurrection of Jesus Christ from the dead. *1 Peter 1:3*

Canticle

Recite the following Canticle, which is hymn, psalm, or song of praise from scriptures.

The Song of Mary   *Magnificat*

Luke 1:46-55

My soul proclaims the greatness of the Lord, my spirit rejoices in God my Savior; for he has looked with favor on his lowly servant. From this day all generations will call me blessed: the Almighty has done great things for me, and holy is his Name. He has mercy on those who fear him in every generation. He has shown the strength of his arm, he has scattered the proud in their conceit. He has cast down the mighty from their thrones, and has lifted up the lowly. He has filled the hungry with good things, and the rich he has sent away empty. He has come to the help of his servant Israel, for he has remembered his promise of mercy, The promise he made to our fathers, to Abraham and his children for ever.

Glory to the Father, and to the Son, and to the Holy Spirit: as it was in the beginning, is now, and will be for ever. *Amen.*

The Apostles' Creed

Read the Apostles Creed. As you recite these words you are acknowledging the universal truths of the Christian faith.

I believe in God, the Father almighty,
creator of heaven and earth;
I believe in Jesus Christ, his only Son, our Lord.
He was conceived by the power of the Holy Spirit
and born of the Virgin Mary.
He suffered under Pontius Pilate,

was crucified, died, and was buried.
He descended to the dead.
On the third day he rose again.
He ascended into heaven,
and is seated at the right hand of the Father.
He will come again to judge the living and the dead.
I believe in the Holy Spirit,
the holy catholic Church,
the communion of saints,
the forgiveness of sins
the resurrection of the body,
and the life everlasting. *Amen.*

The Lord's Prayer

Pray the Lord's Prayer, taking your time and mediating on each line as you pray.

Our Father in heaven,
holy is your Name,
your kingdom come,
your will be done,
on earth as it is in heaven.
Give us this day our daily bread.
Forgive us our sins
as we forgive those
who sin against us.
Lead us not into temptation,

but deliver us from evil.
For yours is the kingdom, the power,
and the glory, forever. *Amen.*

The Intercession

Use the following intercessory prayer to help you focus on specific concerns.

Show us your mercy, O Lord;
And grant us your salvation.
Clothe your ministers with righteousness;
Let your people sing with joy.
Give peace, O Lord, in all the world;
For only in you can we live in safety.
Lord, keep this nation under your care;
And guide us in the way of justice and truth.
Let your way be known upon earth;
Your saving health among all nations.
Let not the needy, O Lord, be forgotten;
Nor the hope of the poor be taken away.
Create in us clean hearts, O God;
And sustain us with your Holy Spirit.

Take some time to pray for yourself and others. Let the Spirit lead you and guide you as you pray.

The Collect

Pray one or more of the following collects.

A Collect for the Renewal of Life

O God, the King eternal, whose light divides the day from the night and turns the shadow of death into the morning: Drive far from us all wrong desires, incline our hearts to keep your law, and guide our feet into the way of peace; that, having done your will with cheerfulness while it was day, we may, when night comes, rejoice to give you thanks; through Jesus Christ our Lord. *Amen.*

A Collect for Peace

O God, the author of peace and lover of concord, to know you is eternal life and to serve you is perfect freedom: Defend us, your humble servants, in all assaults of our enemies; that we, surely trusting in your defense, may not fear the power of any adversaries; through the might of Jesus Christ our Lord. *Amen.*

A Collect for Grace

Lord God, almighty and everlasting Father, you have brought us in safety to this new day: Preserve us with your mighty power, that we may not fall into sin, nor be overcome by adversity; and in all we do, direct us to the fulfilling of your purpose; through Jesus Christ our Lord. *Amen.*

A Collect for Guidance

Heavenly Father, in you we live and move and have our being: We humbly pray you so to guide and govern us by your Holy Spirit, that in all the cares and occupations of our life we may not forget you, but may remember that we are ever walking in your sight; through Jesus Christ our Lord. *Amen.*

The General Thanksgiving

As you prepare to close your time of prayer, you may pray the following thanksgiving or the Prayer of St. John Chrysostom to offer gratitude to God for His many blessings.

Almighty God, Father of all mercies, we your unworthy servants give you humble thanks for all your goodness and loving-kindness to us and to all whom you have made. We bless you for our creation, preservation, and all the blessings of this life; but above all for your immeasurable love in the redemption of the world by our Lord Jesus Christ; for the means of grace, and for the hope of glory. And, we pray, give us such an awareness of your mercies, that with truly thankful hearts we may show forth your praise, not only with our lips, but in our lives, by giving up our selves to your service, and by walking before you in holiness and righteousness all our days; through Jesus Christ our Lord, to whom, with you and the Holy Spirit, be honor and glory throughout all ages. *Amen.*

or

A Prayer of St. Chrysostom

Almighty God, you have given us grace at this time with one accord to make our common supplication to you; and you have promised through your well-beloved Son that when two or three are gathered together in his Name you will be in the midst of them: Fulfill now, O Lord, our desires and petitions as may be best for us; granting us in this world knowledge of your truth, and in the age to come life everlasting. *Amen.*

Benediction

Conclude with one of the following benedictions.

The grace of our Lord Jesus Christ, and the love of God, and the fellowship of the Holy Spirit, be with us all evermore. *Amen. 2 Corinthians 13:14*

May the God of hope fill us with all joy and peace in believing through the power of the Holy Spirit. *Amen.* *Romans 15:13*

Glory to God whose power, working in us, can do infinitely more than we can ask or imagine: Glory to him from generation to generation in the Church, and in Christ Jesus for ever and ever. *Amen. Ephesians 3:20,21*

Evening Prayer

Opening Verses

Read one of the following sentences of Scriptures to prepare your heart for prayer.

Let my prayer be set forth in your sight as incense, the lifting up of my hands as the evening sacrifice. *Psalm 141:2*

Yours is the day, O God, yours also the night; you established the moon and the sun. You fixed all the boundaries of the earth; you made both summer and winter. *Psalm 74:15,16*

I will bless the Lord who gives me counsel; my heart teaches me, night after night. I have set the Lord always before me; because he is at my right hand, I shall not fall. *Psalm 16:7,8*

Confession of Sin

Take a few moments to pray to confession your sins and acknowledge your need for God's grace and forgiveness.

Almighty and most merciful Father,
we have erred and strayed from your ways like lost sheep,
we have followed too much the devices
and desires of our own hearts,
we have offended against your holy laws,
we have left undone those things
which we ought to have done,
and we have done those things
which we ought not to have done.
But you, O Lord, have mercy upon us,
spare those who confess their faults,
restore those who are repentant,
according to your promises declared unto mankind
in Christ Jesus our Lord;
and grant, O most merciful Father, for his sake,
that we may here after live a godly, righteous, and sober
life, to the glory of your holy Name. *Amen.*

End by acknowledging God's mercy and realizing that He has forgiven your sins in Christ Jesus.

May Almighty God have mercy on us, forgive us our sins, through Jesus Christ our Lord, and strengthen us to live in the power of the Holy Spirit, all our days. *Amen.*

The Invitatory

Move to a time of praise by praying the Invitatory and then the Gloria.

O God, make speed to save us. O Lord, make haste to help us.

Glory to the Father, and to the Son, and to the Holy Spirit: as it was in the beginning, is now, and will be for ever. *Amen.*

The Psalm

Read the following Psalm or another one from the Psalter.

Be joyful in the Lord, all you lands; serve the Lord with gladness and come before his presence with a song. Know this: The Lord himself is God; he himself has made us, and we are his; we are his people and the sheep of his pasture. Enter his gates with thanksgiving; go into his courts with praise; give thanks to him and call upon his Name. For the Lord is good; his mercy is everlasting; and his faithfulness endures from age to age. *Psalm 100*

An Evening Prayer

O gracious light,
pure brightness of the everliving Father in heaven,
O Jesus Christ, holy and blessed!

Now as we come to the setting of the sun,
and our eyes behold the vesper light,
we sing your praises, O God: Father, Son, and Holy Spirit.

You are worthy at all times to be praised by happy voices,
O Son of God, O Giver of Life,
and to be glorified through all the worlds.

A Reading

At this time, you may read one or more additional readings from the Old Testament, New Testament, and the Gospels.

It is not ourselves that we proclaim; we proclaim Christ Jesus as Lord, and ourselves as your servants, for Jesus' sake. For the same God who said, "Out of darkness let light shine," has caused his light to shine within us, to give the light of revelation--the revelation of the glory of God in the face of Jesus Christ. *2 Corinthians 4:5-6*

Canticle

Recite the following Canticle, which is hymn, psalm, or song of praise from scriptures.

The Song of Simeon   Nunc Dimittis

Luke 2:29-32

Lord, you now have set your servant free to go in peace as you have promised; For these eyes of mine have seen the Savior, whom you have prepared for all the world to see: A Light to enlighten the nations, and the glory of your people Israel.

Glory to the Father, and to the Son, and to the Holy Spirit: as it was in the beginning, is now, and will be for ever. *Amen.*

The Apostles' Creed

Read the Apostles Creed. As you recite these words you are acknowledging the universal truths of the Christian faith.

I believe in God, the Father almighty,
creator of heaven and earth;
I believe in Jesus Christ, his only Son, our Lord.
He was conceived by the power of the Holy Spirit

and born of the Virgin Mary.
He suffered under Pontius Pilate,
was crucified, died, and was buried.
He descended to the dead.
On the third day he rose again.
He ascended into heaven,
and is seated at the right hand of the Father.
He will come again to judge the living and the dead.
I believe in the Holy Spirit,
the holy catholic Church,
the communion of saints,
the forgiveness of sins
the resurrection of the body,
and the life everlasting. *Amen.*

The Lord's Prayer

Pray the Lord's Prayer, taking your time and mediating on each line as you pray.

Our Father in heaven,
holy is your Name,
your kingdom come,
your will be done,
on earth as it is in heaven.
Give us this day our daily bread.
Forgive us our sins
as we forgive those

who sin against us.
Lead us not into temptation,
but deliver us from evil.
For yours is the kingdom, the power,
and the glory, forever. *Amen.*

The Intercession

*Use the following intercessory prayer to help you
focus on specific concerns.*

Make your ways known upon earth, Lord God,
your saving power among all peoples.
Renew your Church in holiness
and help us to serve you with joy.
Guide the leaders of all nations,
that justice may prevail throughout the world.
Let not the needy be forgotten,
nor the hope of the poor be taken away.
Make us instruments of your peace
and let your glory be over all the earth. *Amen*

*Take some time to pray for yourself and others. Let the Spirit lead
you and guide you as you pray.*

The Collect

Pray one or more of the following collects.

A Collect for Peace

Most holy God, the source of all good desires, all right
judgements, and all just works: Give to us, your servants,
that peace which the world cannot give, so that our minds
may be fixed on the doing of your will, and that we, being
delivered from the fear of all enemies, may live in peace
and quietness; through the mercies of Christ Jesus our
Savior. *Amen.*

A Collect for Aid against Perils

Be our light in the darkness, O Lord, and in your great
mercy defend us from all perils and dangers of this night;
for the love of your only Son, our Savior Jesus Christ.
Amen.

A Collect for the Presence of Christ

Lord Jesus, stay with us, for evening is at hand and the day
is past; be our companion in the way, kindle our hearts,
and awaken hope, that we may know you as you are
revealed in Scripture and the breaking of bread. Grant this
for the sake of your love. *Amen.*

The General Thanksgiving

As you prepare to close your time of prayer, you may pray the following thanksgiving or the Prayer of St. John Chrysostom to offer gratitude to God for His many blessings.

Almighty God, Father of all mercies, we your unworthy servants give you humble thanks for all your goodness and loving-kindness to us and to all whom you have made. We bless you for our creation, preservation, and all the blessings of this life; but above all for your immeasurable love in the redemption of the world by our Lord Jesus Christ; for the means of grace, and for the hope of glory. And, we pray, give us such an awareness of your mercies, that with truly thankful hearts we may show forth your praise, not only with our lips, but in our lives, by giving up our selves to your service, and by walking before you in holiness and righteousness all our days; through Jesus Christ our Lord, to whom, with you and the Holy Spirit, be honor and glory throughout all ages. *Amen.*

or

A Prayer of St. Chrysostom

Almighty God, you have given us grace at this time with one accord to make our common supplication to you; and you have promised through your well-beloved Son that when two or three are gathered together in his Name you will be in the midst of them: Fulfill now, O Lord, our desires and petitions as may be best for us; granting us in this world knowledge of your truth, and in the age to come life everlasting. *Amen.*

Benediction

Conclude with one of the following benedictions.

The grace of our Lord Jesus Christ, and the love of God, and the fellowship of the Holy Spirit, be with us all evermore. *Amen. 2 Corinthians 13:14*

May the God of hope fill us with all joy and peace in believing through the power of the Holy Spirit. *Amen. Romans 15:13*

Glory to God whose power, working in us, can do infinitely more than we can ask or imagine: Glory to him from generation to generation in the Church, and in Christ Jesus for ever and ever. *Amen. Ephesians 3:20,21*

Chapter 2

THANKS BE TO GOD
Prayers for Various Occasions

"Years ago when I wanted to become more skillful in public prayer, I was fortunate to come across the collects of Thomas Cranmer, the writer of the original Episcopal Book of Common Prayer." -Tim Keller

Prayer is as essential to the spiritual life as air is to our lungs or water is to the body. For that reason, there is nothing more universal than the practice of prayer. If you think about it, prayer is one of the practices that Christians share in common around the world. There are people praying on every continent and every nation. One day in the not so distant future, the Bible tells us that every knee will bow and every tongue will confess that Jesus is Lord (Romans 14:11).

In every age, men and women have talked with God in prayer. Prayer is God's way of communicating with His people. It is the primary way that we build a relationship with God the Father, Jesus Christ the Son, and the Holy Spirit. Prayer brings us into direct communion with the Lord.

Some people think prayer is something they have to do just like checking something off a "to do" list. But that really isn't prayer at all. We should think of prayer in intimate terms, like a conversation between close friends. What are some words that you think of when you think of an intimate friendship? You will probably think of words like loving, caring, warm, sincere, personal, and intimate. These are words that should be used to describe our prayer time with the Lord. Prayer should not be dry or stuffy; it should be warm and intimate.

Prayer doesn't change God- prayer changes us. C.S. Lewis said, "I pray because I can't help myself. I pray because I'm helpless. I pray because the need flows out of me all the time- waking and sleeping. It doesn't change God- it changes me." Through prayer we are changed and transformed into the image and likeness of Jesus Christ. To pray means that we must be open and willing to change. We are changed as we gain a greater awareness of Christ and learn what His will is for our lives.

I am a firm believer that prayer is not something that can be taught in a classroom; it must be learned through practice, repetition, and trial and error. Like an artist who spends years learning their craft, so a believer must commit themselves to a life-long pursuit of learning how to pray. Just as a baby learns how to walk with tiny steps, or a child learns how to ride a bicycle with training wheels, we learn to pray by praying. There is no magic to it; we just pray.

There are times when we simply don't have the words to express ourselves in prayer. When we don't know how to pray or when we need encouragement to pray, we look to the church. The prayers of fellow Christians can inspire and encourage us whenever we find ourselves at a loss for words or when our desire to pray is not there. Many prayers and thanksgivings have been recorded and passed down since the days of the Bible to be used by others for mutual encouragement. Throughout the ages, Christians have continued to write down prayers to be used at different times and for different occasions so that other Christians may share them as well.

This section of *Our Common Prayer* contains a collection of written ancient and contemporary prayers and thanksgivings for various occasions. Prayer helps us celebrate life- from birth to death. These prayers have been drawn from the Book of Common Prayer and are written in our contemporary English language. In the following pages, you will find a prayer for just about any need. You will find yourself falling in love with these beautiful prayers and returning to them throughout the day.

Prayer for Various Occasions

For Guidance

Direct us, O Lord, in all our doings with your most gracious favor, and further us with your continual help; that in all our works begun, continued, and ended in you, we may glorify your holy Name, and finally, by your mercy, obtain everlasting life; through Jesus Christ our Lord. *Amen.*

For Peace

O God, the author of peace and lover of concord, to know you is eternal life and to serve you is perfect freedom: Defend us, your humble servants, in all assaults of our enemies; that we, surely trusting in your defense, may not fear the power of any adversaries; through the might of Jesus Christ our Lord. *Amen.*

For the Renewal of Life

O God, the King eternal, whose light divides the day from the night and turns the shadow of death into the morning: Drive far from us all wrong desires, incline our hearts to keep your law, and guide our feet into the way of peace; that, having done your will with cheerfulness while it was day, we may, when night comes, rejoice to give you thanks; through Jesus Christ our Lord. *Amen.*

Prayer for Purity

Almighty God, to you all hearts are open, all desires known,and from you no secrets are hid: Cleanse the thoughts of our hearts by the inspiration of your Holy

Spirit, that we may perfectly love you, and worthily magnify your holy Name; through Christ our Lord. *Amen.*

For Quiet Confidence

O God of peace, who has taught us that in returning and rest we shall be saved, in quietness and confidence shall be our strength: By the might of your Spirit lift us, we pray, to your presence, where we may be still and know that you are God; through Jesus Christ our Lord. *Amen.*

For Protection

Assist us mercifully, O Lord, in these our supplications and prayers, and dispose the way of your servants towards the attainment of everlasting salvation; that, among all the changes and chances of this mortal life, they may ever be defended by your gracious and ready help; through Jesus Christ our Lord. *Amen.*

An Evening Prayer

Lord Jesus, stay with us, for evening is at hand and the day is past; be our companion in the way, kindle our hearts, and awaken hope, that we may know you as you are revealed in Scripture and the breaking of bread. Grant this for the sake of your love. *Amen.*

A Confession of Sin

Most merciful God, we confess that we have sinned
against you in thought, word, and deed, by what we have
done, and by what we have left undone. We have not
loved you with our whole heart; we have not loved our
neighbors as ourselves. We are truly sorry and we humbly
repent. For the sake of your Son Jesus Christ, have mercy
on us and forgive us; that we may delight in your will, and
walk in your ways, to the glory of your Name. *Amen.*

A Prayer of Self-Dedication

Almighty and eternal God, so draw our hearts to you, so
guide our minds, so fill our imaginations, so control our
wills, that we may be wholly yours, utterly dedicated unto
you; and then use us, we pray, as you will, and always to
your glory and the welfare of your people; through our
Lord and Savior Jesus Christ. *Amen.*

A Prayer attributed to St. Francis

Lord, make us instruments of your peace. Where there is
hatred, let us sow love; where there is injury, pardon;
where there is discord, union; where there is doubt, faith;
where there is despair, hope; where there is darkness, light;
where there is sadness, joy. Grant that we may not so much
seek to be consoled as to console; to be understood as to

understand; to be loved as to love. For it is in giving that we receive; it is in pardoning that we are pardoned; and it is in dying that we are born to eternal life. *Amen.*

For God's Healing

O God, the source of all health: So fill my heart with faith in your love, that with calm expectancy I may make room for your power to possess me, and gracefully accept your healing; through Jesus Christ our Lord. *Amen.*

In Pain

Lord Jesus Christ, by your patience in suffering you hallowed earthly pain and gave us the example of obedience to your Father's will: Be near me in my time of weakness and pain; sustain me by your grace, that my strength and courage may not fail; heal me according to your will; and help me always to believe that what happens to me here is of little account if you hold me in eternal life, my Lord and my God. *Amen.*

In the Evening

O Lord, support us all the day long, until the shadows lengthen, and the evening comes, and the busy world is hushed, and the fever of life is over, and our work is done. Then in your mercy, grant us a safe lodging, and a holy rest, and peace at the last. *Amen.*

Before Worship

O Almighty God, who pours out on all who desire it the spirit of grace and of supplication: Deliver us, when we draw near to you, from coldness of heart and wanderings of mind, that with steadfast thoughts and kindled affections we may worship you in spirit and in truth; through Jesus Christ our Lord. *Amen.*

Before Communion

Be present, be present, O Jesus, our great High Priest, as you were present with your disciples, and be know to us in the breaking of bread; who live and reign with the Father and the Holy Spirit, now and for ever. *Amen.*

After Communion

Almighty God, Holy Father, we have sat at your feet, learned from your word, and eaten from your table. We give you thanks and praise for accepting us into your family. Send us out with your blessing, to live and to witness for you in the power of your Spirit, through Jesus Christ, the first born from the dead. *Amen.*

After Worship

Grant, we pray, Almighty God, that the words which we have heard this day with our outward ears, may, through your grace, be so grafted inwardly in our hearts, that they may bring forth in us the fruit of good living, to the honor and praise of your Name; through Jesus Christ our Lord. *Amen.*

On Sunday

O God our King, by the resurrection of your Son Jesus Christ on the first day of the week, you conquered sin, put death to light, and gave us the hope of everlasting life: Redeem all our days by this victory; forgive our sins, banish our fears, make us bold to praise you and to do your will; and steel us to wait for the consummation of your kingdom on the last great Day; through the same Jesus Christ our Lord. *Amen.*

Grace at Meals

Blessed are you, O Lord God, for you give us food to sustain our lives and make our hearts glad. Give us grateful hearts for all your blessings, and make us mindful of the needs of others; through Jesus Christ our Lord. *Amen.*

A House Blessing

Heavenly Father, of whom the whole family in heaven and earth is named; Be present in this house, that all who live here, being kindly affectionate one to another, may find it a place of blessing and of peace; through Jesus Christ our Lord. *Amen.*

Chapter 3

LORD HEAR OUR PRAYERS
Prayers for the Sake of Others

"There is nothing that makes us love a man so much as praying for him."
-William Law

There are literally millions of people who are living in poverty in the shadow of our nation's great wealth. Hunger and poverty are quickly becoming a serious epidemic in the United States. Every month, close to twenty million Americans go hungry. According to the census, over thirty five million people live below the poverty line, up 1.3 million from 2002. Most of our nation's poor are children and the elderly. There are over 50,000 orphaned children in America. There are many more people in every city of our nation who are homeless and can't even provide basic needs such as food and clothing. In addition, drugs, domestic violence, and illiteracy are harsh realities for many people.

Who are these people in need? Where do they live? Where can we find them? They are in our cities, communities, and small towns. They are our neighbors, fellow church members, and even family members. They are not numbers or mere statistics, but they have names, faces, and feelings. More importantly, they have real needs that can be met by the church.

As Christians, we are called to pray not only for ourselves, but to pray for others- the church, the hurting, the sick, and the world in which we live. The call to pray for others flows from the command to love our neighbors. Jesus said, "Love your neighbor as yourself" (Matthew 22:36-40, NIV). We pray because we love, and we love because God first loved us. Love flows from Him to all His creation. John reminds us, "This is love: not that we loved God, but that he loved us and sent his Son as an atoning sacrifice for our sins" (1 John 4:10, NIV). Love begins and ends with God, and flows from us to our neighbors through our prayers.

To pray for others is commonly called "intercessory prayer." The Scriptures are full of examples that show us that God desires us to pray for others. God said, "And I searched for a man among them who should build up the wall and stand in the gap before Me for the land, that I should not destroy it; but I found no one" (Ezekiel 22:30-31, NASB). There are numerous other examples of people in the Bible who interceded on behalf of others, but the greatest example of intercession can be seen in the life and ministry of Jesus Christ. The Bible tells us, "He always lives to make intercession" (Hebrews 7:25, ESV). Jesus sits at the right hand of God and continually makes intercession on our behalf. Jesus' intercession isn't just a prayer that He prayed, but the life He lived for you and for me.

Everything that Jesus said and did was not for Himself; it was all for us! His whole life was an intercession. The Bible tells us, "For there is one God, and there is one mediator between God and men, the man Christ Jesus" (1 Timothy 2:5, ESV). True intercession begins by following Jesus' example of loving and serving others that flows into fervent prayer for the lives of others.

Intercessory prayer has always been an important part of the life and ministry of the church. One of the earliest forms of intercessory prayer is called the litany or bidding prayer, where the person leading in prayer makes a specific prayer request and the people who were gathered would respond with a sentence or phrase, such as "Lord, hear our prayer," or "Lord, have mercy."

In the following prayers for the sake of others, you will find prayers for almost any need or occasion: prayers for the nation; prayers for social justice; prayers for the weather; prayers for the poor and neglected; even prayers for musicians and artists. You can use the following forms of intercessory prayers as an aid to help guide you to pray for the needs of others. As you do, you will be reminded of the simple, yet powerful gift of intercessory prayer.

Prayers for the Sake of Others

Prayers for Others

For Families

Almighty God, our heavenly Father, we commend to your continual care the homes in which your people dwell. Put far from them, we pray, every root of bitterness, the desire of vainglory, and the pride of life. Fill them with faith, virtue, knowledge, temperance, patience, godliness. Knit together in constant affection those who, in holy marriage, have been made one flesh. Turn the hearts of the parents to the children, and the hearts of the children to the parents; and so enkindle fervent love among us all, that we may evermore be kindly affectioned one to another; through Jesus Christ our Lord. *Amen.*

For the Care of Children

Almighty God, heavenly Father, you have blessed us with the joy and care of children: Give us calm strength and patient wisdom as we bring them up, that we may teach them to love whatever is just and true and good, following the example of our Savior Jesus Christ. *Amen.*

For Young Persons

God our Father, you see your children growing up in an
unsteady and confusing world: Show them that your ways
give more life than the ways of the world, and that
following you is better than chasing after selfish goals.
Help them to take failure, not as a measure of their worth,
but as a chance for a new start. Give them strength to hold
their faith in you, and to keep alive their joy in your
creation; through Jesus Christ our Lord. *Amen.*

For the Gift of a Child

Heavenly Father, you sent; your own Son into this world.
We thank you for the life of this child, *N.*, entrusted to our
care. Help us to remember that we are all your children,
and so to love and nurture *him*, that *he* may attain to that
full stature intended for *him* in your eternal kingdom; for
the sake of your dear Son, Jesus Christ our Lord. *Amen.*

For Travelers

O God, our heavenly Father, whose glory fills the whole
creation, and whose presence we find wherever we go:
Preserve those who travel; surround them with your
loving care; protect them from every danger; and bring
them in safety to their journey's end; through Jesus Christ
our Lord. Amen.

Prayers for Those Who Mourn

O God, who brought us to birth, and in whose arms we die, in our grief and shock contain and comfort us; embrace us with your love, give us hope in our confusion and grace to let go into new life; through Jesus Christ. *Amen.*

For Those Who Live Alone

Almighty God, whose Son had nowhere to lay his head: Grant that those who live alone may not be lonely in their solitude, but that, following in his steps, they may find fulfillment in loving you and their neighbors; through Jesus Christ our Lord. *Amen.*

For the Aged

Look with mercy, O God our Father, on all whose increasing years bring them weakness, distress, or isolation. Provide for them homes of dignity and peace; give them understanding helpers, and the willingness to accept help; and, as their strength diminishes, increase their faith and their assurance of your love. This we ask in the name of Jesus Christ our Lord. *Amen.*

For a Birthday

O God, our times are in your hand: Look with favor, we pray, on you servant *N.* as *he* begins another year. Grant that *he* may grow in wisdom and grace, and strengthen *his* trust in your goodness all the days of *his* life; through Jesus Christ our Lord. *Amen.*

For those we Love

Almighty God, we entrust all who are dear to us to your never-failing care and love, for this life and the life to come, knowing that you are doing for them better things than we can desire or pray for; through Jesus Christ our Lord. *Amen.*

For the Victims of Addiction

O blessed Lord, you ministered to all who came to you: Look with compassion upon all who through addiction have lost their health and freedom. Restore to them the assurance of your unfailing mercy; remove from them the fears that beset them; strengthen them in the work of their recovery; and to those who care for them, give patient understanding and persevering love. *Amen.*

Prayers for the Church

For the Mission of the Church

Almighty God, you sent your Son Jesus Christ to reconcile
the world to yourself: We praise and bless you for those
whom you have sent in the power of the Spirit to preach
the Gospel to all nations. We thank you that in all parts of
the earth a community of love has been gathered together
by their prayers and labors, and that in every place your
servants call upon your Name; for the kingdom and the
power and the glory are yours for ever. *Amen.*

For the Church

Gracious Father, we pray for the holy Catholic Church. Fill
it with all truth, in all truth with all peace. Where it is
corrupt, purify it; where it is in error, direct it; where in
any thing it is amiss, reform it. Where it is right, strengthen
it; where it is in want, provide for it; where it is divided,
reunite it; for the sake of Jesus Christ thy Son our Savior.
Amen.

For the Mission of the Church

Everliving God, whose will it is that all should come to
you through your Son Jesus Christ: Inspire our witness to
him, that all may know the power of his forgiveness and

the hope of his resurrection; who lives and reigns with you
and the Holy Spirit, one God, now and for ever. *Amen.*

For a Local Church

Almighty and everliving God, ruler of all things in heaven
and earth, hear our prayers for this church family.
Strengthen the faithful, arouse the careless, and restore the
broken hearted. Grant us all things necessary for our
common life, and bring us all to be of one heart and mind
within your holy Church; through Jesus Christ our Lord.
Amen.

For the Unity of the Church

O God the Father of our Lord Jesus Christ, our only Savior,
the Prince of Peace: Give us grace to lay to heart the great
dangers we are in by our unhappy divisions; take away all
hatred and prejudice, and whatever else may hinder us
from godly union and concord; that, as there is but one
Body and one Spirit, one hope of our calling, one Lord, one
Faith, one Baptism, one God and Father of us all, so we
may be all of one heart and of one soul, united in one holy
bond of truth and peace, of faith and charity, and may with
one mind and one mouth glorify you; through Jesus Christ
our Lord. *Amen.*

For those about to be Baptized or to renew their Baptismal Covenant

O God, you prepared your disciples for the coming of the Spirit through the teaching of your Son Jesus Christ: Make the hearts and minds of your servants ready to receive the blessing of the Holy Spirit, that they may be filled with the strength of his presence; through Jesus Christ our Lord. *Amen.*

For Church Musicians and Artists

O God, whom saints and angels delight to worship in heaven: Be ever present with your servants who seek through art and music to perfect the praises offered by your people on earth; and grant to them even now glimpses of your beauty, and make them worthy at length to behold it unveiled for evermore; through Jesus Christ our Lord. *Amen.*

Prayers for Society

For our Country

Almighty God, who hast given us this good land for our heritage: Bless our land with honorable industry, sound learning, and pure manners. Save us from violence, discord, and confusion; from pride and arrogance, and from every evil way. Defend our liberties, and fashion into one united people the multitudes brought hither out of many kindreds and tongues. Endue with the spirit of wisdom those to whom in thy Name we entrust the authority of government, that there may be justice and peace at home, and that, through obedience to thy law, we may show forth thy praise among the nations of the earth. In the time of prosperity, fill our hearts with thankfulness, and in the day of trouble, suffer not our trust in thee to fail; all which we ask through Jesus Christ our Lord. *Amen.*

For the President of the United States and all in Civil Authority

O Lord our Governor, whose glory is in all the world: We commend this nation to your merciful care, that, being guided by your Providence, we may dwell secure in your peace. Grant to the President of the United States and to all in authority, wisdom and strength to know and to do your will. Fill them with the love of truth and righteousness, and make them ever mindful of their calling to serve this people; through Jesus Christ our Lord, who lives and reigns with you and the Holy Spirit, one God, world without end. *Amen.*

For Local Government

Almighty God our heavenly Father, send down upon those who hold office in this State (City, County, Town,

_____) the spirit of wisdom, charity, and justice; that with steadfast purpose they may faithfully serve in their offices to promote the well-being of all people; through Jesus Christ our Lord. *Amen.*

For an Election

Almighty God, to whom we must account for all our powers and privileges: Guide the people of the United States (*or* of this community) in the election of officials and representatives; that, by faithful administration and wise laws, the rights of all may be protected and our nation be enabled to fulfill your purposes; through Jesus Christ our Lord. *Amen.*

For those in the Armed Forces of our Country

Almighty God, we commend to your gracious care and keeping all the men and women of our armed forces at home and abroad. Defend them day by day with your heavenly grace; strengthen them in their trials and temptations; give them courage to face the perils which beset them; and grant them a sense of your abiding presence wherever they may be; through Jesus Christ our Lord. *Amen.*

For those who suffer for the sake of Conscience

O God our Father, whose Son forgave his enemies while he was suffering shame and death: Strengthen those who suffer for the sake of conscience; when they are accused, save them from speaking in hate; when they are rejected, save them from bitterness; when they are imprisoned, save them from despair; and to us your servants, give grace to respect their witness and to discern the truth, that our society may be cleansed and strengthened. This we ask for the sake of Jesus Christ, our merciful and righteous Judge. *Amen.*

For Social Justice

Grant, O God, that your holy and life-giving Spirit may so move every human heart [and especially the hearts of the people of this land], that barriers which divide us may crumble, suspicions disappear, and hatreds cease; that our divisions being healed, we may live in justice and peace; through Jesus Christ our Lord. *Amen.*

In Times of Conflict

O God, you have bound us together in a common life. Help us, in the midst of our struggles for justice and truth, to confront one another without hatred or bitterness, and to work together with mutual forbearance and respect; through Jesus Christ our Lord. *Amen.*

For Agriculture

Almighty God, we thank you for making the earth fruitful, so that it might produce what is needed for life: Bless those who work in the fields; give us seasonable weather; and grant that we may all share the fruits for the earth, rejoicing in your goodness; through Jesus Christ our Lord. *Amen.*

For the Unemployed

Heavenly Father, we remember before you those who suffer want and anxiety from lack of work. Guide the people of this land so to use our public and private wealth that all may find suitable and fulfilling employment, and receive just payment for their labor; through Jesus Christ our Lord. *Amen.*

For Schools and Colleges

O Eternal God, bless all schools, colleges, and universities [and especially _____], that they may be lively centers for sound learning, new discovery, and the pursuit of wisdom; and grant that those who teach and those who

learn may find you to be the source of all truth; through
Jesus Christ our Lord. *Amen.*

For the Good Use of Leisure

O God, in the course of this busy life, give us times of
refreshment and peace; and grant that we may so use our
leisure to rebuild our bodies and renew our minds, that
our spirits may be opened to the goodness of your
creation; through Jesus Christ our Lord. *Amen.*

For Cities

Heavenly Father, in your Word you have given us a vision
of that holy City to which the nations of the world bring
their glory: Behold and visit, we pray, the cities of the
earth. Renew the ties of mutual regard which form our
civic life. Send us honest and able leaders. Enable us to
eliminate poverty, prejudice, and oppression, that peace
may prevail with righteousness, and justice with order,
and that men and women from different cultures and with
differing talents may find with one another the fulfillment
of their humanity; through Jesus Christ our Lord. *Amen.*

For the Poor and the Neglected

Almighty and most merciful God, we remember before
you all poor and neglected persons whom it would be easy

for us to forget: the homeless and the destitute, the old and the sick, and all who have none to care for them. Help us to heal those who are broken in body or spirit, and to turn their sorrow into joy. Grant this, Father, for the love of your Son, who for our sake became poor, Jesus Christ our Lord. *Amen.*

For the Oppressed

Look with pity, O heavenly Father, upon the people in this land who live with injustice, terror, disease, and death as their constant companions. Have mercy upon us. Help us to eliminate our cruelty to these our neighbors. Strengthen those who spend their lives establishing equal protection of the law and equal opportunities for all. And grant that every one of us may enjoy a fair portion of the riches of this land; through Jesus Christ our Lord. *Amen.*

For the Right Use of God's Gifts

Almighty God, whose loving hand has given us all that we possess: Grant us grace that we may honor you with our substance, and, remembering the account which we must one day give, may be faithful stewards of your bounty, through Jesus Christ our Lord. *Amen.*

Prayers for the World

For Peace in Our World

Make your ways known upon earth, Lord God, your
saving power among all peoples. Renew your Church in
holiness and help us to serve you with joy. Guide the
leaders of all nations, that justice may prevail throughout
the world. Let not the needy be forgotten, nor the hope of
the poor be taken away. Make us instruments of your
peace and let your glory be over all the earth. *Amen.*

For Joy in God's Creation

O heavenly Father, who has filled the world with beauty:
Open our eyes to behold your gracious hand in all your
works; that, rejoicing in your whole creation, we may learn
to serve you with gladness; for the sake of him through
whom all things were made, your Son Jesus Christ our
Lord. *Amen.*

For the Diversity of Races and Cultures

O God, who created all peoples in your image, we thank
you for the wonderful diversity of races and cultures in
this world. Enrich our lives by ever-widening circles of
fellowship, and show us your presence in those who differ
most from us, until our knowledge of your love is made

perfect in our love for all your children; through Jesus
Christ our Lord. *Amen.*

For Peace

Eternal God, in whose perfect kingdom no sword is drawn
but the sword of righteousness, no strength known but the
strength of love: So mightily spread abroad your Spirit,
that all peoples may be gathered under the banner of the
Prince of Peace, as children of one Father; to whom be
dominion and glory, now and for ever. *Amen.*

For Peace Among the Nations

Almighty God our heavenly Father, guide the nations of
the world into the way of justice and truth, and establish
among them that peace which is the fruit of righteousness,
that they may become the kingdom of our Lord and Savior
Jesus Christ. *Amen.*

For our Enemies

O God, the Father of all, whose Son commanded us to love
our enemies: Lead them and us from prejudice to truth:
deliver them and us from hatred, cruelty, and revenge; and
in your good time enable us all to stand reconciled before
you, through Jesus Christ our Lord. *Amen.*

Prayers for the Sick

For Healing

Heavenly Father, giver of life and health: Comfort and
relieve N., and give your power of healing to those who
minister to *his* needs, that *he* may be strengthened in *his*
weakness and have confidence in your loving care;
through Jesus Christ our Lord. *Amen.*

For a Sick Child

Lord Jesus Christ, Good Shepherd of the sheep, you gather
the lambs in your arms and carry them in your bosom: We
commend to your loving care this child N. Relieve *his*
pain, guard *him* from all danger, restore to *him* your gifts of
gladness and strength, and raise *him* up to a life of service
to you. Hear us, we pray, for you dear Name's sake. *Amen.*

For Health of Body and Soul

May God the Father bless you, God the Son heal you, God
the Holy Spirit give you strength. May God the holy and
undivided Trinity guard your body, save your soul, and
bring you safely to his heavenly country; where he lives
and reigns for ever and ever. *Amen.*

Chapter 4

WE BELIEVE
The Creeds of the Christian Faith

"Our calling is not to reinvent the Christian faith, but, in keeping with the past, to carry forward what the church has affirmed from the beginning." -Robert Webber

The world is changing all around us. The old pathways of modernity are collapsing and the new world of postmodernism is emerging. The postmodern paradigm shift can be compared to previous time periods such as the Reformation or the Age of Reason. Author Leonard Sweet says, "The seismic events that have happened in the aftermath of the postmodern earthquake have generated tidal waves that have created a whole new world." Futurists, theologians, and philosophers call this new world "postmodernism."

There is no shortage of spirituality in our new postmodern world. The postmodern world is a very spiritual place where people are looking for a spirituality that is real and relevant, a spirituality that is not dead and outdated. Many people in North America are increasingly seeking spirituality outside of the traditional church by looking to alternative religions. Buddhism and other eastern religions are experiencing explosive growth in

North America and around the world. In the marketplace of consumer spirituality, individuals are not choosing one religion over the other; rather, they are weaving together their own patchwork spirituality.

Christianity has its own unique form of spirituality, but what makes it stand out from our postmodern world is that we actually believe in something, or more importantly, Someone. Faith in God matters because what we believe about God influences how we think, pray, worship, and, ultimately, how we live.

Although we are not all called to be theologians, all Christians have a responsibility to know what they believe for themselves because what we believe influences how we worship. Think about it: you cannot worship what you don't know. There is an old latin phrase *"Lex orandi, lex credendi,"* which is translated "the law of prayer is the law of belief." This reminds us that prayer shapes our beliefs and our beliefs ultimately shape our prayer.

Perhaps you are thinking, "Why would you include a chapter on Creeds in a book about prayer?" Since the earliest of times, Christians have recited creeds during times of prayer and worship to remind them of the faith that they professed. The church in every generation is commanded to, "contend for the faith that was once for all delivered to the saints" (Jude 3, ESV). We do not need to reinvent our faith; we need to get back to the basics of Christianity. Every generation of believers should revisit the passionate faith and doctrine of the early church as found in the creeds.

So what is a creed? A creed is a brief statement of faith used to clarify doctrinal points and to distinguish truth from error. The word *creed* comes from the Latin word *credo*, meaning, "I believe." The Bible contains a number of creed-like passages (Deuteronomy 6:4-9, 1 Corinthians 8:6; 12:3; 15:3-4; 1 Timothy 3:16). The creeds offer us a concise summary of authentic Christian doctrine.

As the early church spread, there was a practical need for a statement of faith to help believers focus on the most important doctrines of their Christian faith. The Apostles' Creed is named not because the original apostles wrote it, but because it accurately reflects the teaching of the apostles. The final text of the Apostles' Creed was eventually accepted around 800 AD as the standard form in the Western church (see my book *Creed: Connect to the Basic Essentials of Historic Christian Faith*, 2011).

As the church continued to grow, heresies also grew, and the early Christians needed to clarify the defining boundaries of the faith. In the early 300's, controversy developed over the divinity of Jesus Christ. At the request of Emperor Constantine, Christian bishops from across the East and the West met at the town of Nicea, near Constantinople. In 325 AD they wrote an expanded creed, called the Creed of Nicea. These two creeds are widely accepted among all Christians as statements of true Christian orthodoxy.

Our creeds are not static statements about the Christian faith, rather they offer the Church a dynamic means of unity in the essentials of our common faith. The creeds are meant to guard our faith, not limit the sovereign leading of the Holy Spirit. With the creeds as a foundation, we can be open to the diversity that is in the various Church traditions. Our unity in essentials gives us common ground, while our diversity provides us the means for various dialogues and opinions within the body of Christ. With the creeds as our foundation, the church of the past can speak to the present, and the church of the present can reach into the future through a common faith and a common prayer.

The creeds fill the pages of the Book of Common Prayer and is infused throughout its prayers, liturgies, ceremonies, and catechism. In many ways, the creeds act as an anchor that provides a doctrinal foundation for the Book of Common Prayer.

Here are the Apostles' and Nicene Creeds. You can use them during times of prayer, devotion, or personal reflection on the content of our common faith. I have also included the Baptismal Creed and short trinitarian affirmation of the faith based upon the historic creeds.

The Apostles' Creed

I believe in God, the Father almighty,

creator of heaven and earth;

I believe in Jesus Christ, his only Son, our Lord.

He was conceived by the power of the Holy Spirit
and born of the Virgin Mary.

He suffered under Pontius Pilate,
was crucified, died, and was buried.

He descended to the dead.

On the third day he rose again.

He ascended into heaven,
and is seated at the right hand of the Father.

He will come again to judge the living and the dead.

I believe in the Holy Spirit,
the holy catholic Church,
the communion of saints,
the forgiveness of sins
the resurrection of the body,
and the life everlasting. *Amen.*

The Nicene Creed

We believe in one God
the Father, the Almighty,
creator of heaven and earth,
and of all that is, seen and unseen.

We believe in one Lord, Jesus Christ,
 the only Son of God,
eternally begotten of the Father,

God from God, Light from Light,
true God from true God,
begotten, not made,
of one being with the Father.
Through him all things were made.
For us men and for our salvation
he came down from heaven;
by the power of the Holy Spirit
he became incarnate from the Virgin Mary,
and was made man.
For our sake he was crucified under Pontius Pilate;
he suffered death and was buried.
On the third day he rose again in accordance with the
Scriptures;
he ascended into heaven
and is seated at the right hand of the Father.
He will come again in glory
to judge the living and the dead,
and his kingdom will have no end.
We believe in the Holy Spirit,
the Lord, the giver of life,
who proceeds from the Father (and the Son).
With the Father and the Son he is worshipped
and glorified.
He has spoken through the Prophets.
We believe in one, holy, catholic,
and apostolic Church.
We acknowledge one baptism

for the forgiveness of sins.
We look for the resurrection of the dead,
and the life of the world to come. *Amen.*

Baptismal Creed

Do you believe in God, the Father almighty,
creator of heaven and earth.
I do.

Do you believe in Jesus Christ, his only Son, our Lord.
He was conceived by the power of the Holy Spirit
and born of the Virgin Mary.
He suffered under Pontius Pilate,
was crucified, died, and was buried.
He descended to the dead.
On the third day he rose again.
He ascended into heaven,
and is seated at the right hand of the Father.
He will come again to judge the living and the dead.
I do.

Do you believe in God the Holy Spirit,
the holy catholic Church,
the communion of saints,
the forgiveness of sins,
the resurrection of the body,
and the life everlasting.

I do.

Affirmation of the Faith

I believe in God the Father, Almighty.
I believe in Jesus Christ, His Only Son.
I believe in the Holy Spirit, Giver of Life.
I believe in the Three in One. *Amen.*

Chapter 5

ALL SAINTS
Prayers of the Saints

"For all the saints who from their labors rest, Who thee by faith before the world confess, Thy name, O Jesus, be forever blest, Alleluia! Alleluia!" -William W. How

We live in a wordy world where words have virtually lost their meaning. This is due in part to an overabundance of words. You can't escape them because they are everywhere. Words in print. Words on signs. Words on billboards. Words on TV, computer, Facebook, Twitter, text messages: need I go on? The average American is bombarded with over 3,000 advertising messages a day! The Bible warns us, "In the multitude of words sin is not lacking" (Proverbs 10:19, NKJV).

Even though words are everywhere, we have become desensitized to their importance, especially when it comes to the spoken word. This has led to a breakdown in communication in our society. With the proliferation of words has come the rise of social media, like Facebook and Twitter, where you can have thousands of friends and followers. The result: talk is cheap, and relationships are superficial. People would rather text than talk. In spite all of our communication and technological advances, people are more depressed and lonely than ever before.

The devaluing of words has also had a profound effect on how we pray and communicate with God. Many of our prayers are shallow, selfish, and lack any serious reflection upon the nature of God and the suffering of others. We don't need prayers that are longer or louder; we need ones that are more thoughtful and focused on God and His kingdom.

If history can teach us anything, it is the value and the importance of words. In particular, church history reminds us that words matter to God; therefore, they should matter to us. The Bible tells us, "In the beginning was the Word, and the Word was with God, and the Word was God" (John 1:1, ESV). God's spoken Word created the entire universe and everything in it. In the beginning God spoke His Word and we have been speaking back to Him in prayer every since. God has ordained words to be the means of communion with Him. Prayer is our humble attempt to use words to respond to the God who spoke the world into existence.

There is a great prayer tradition that goes back to Moses, David, Jesus, and Paul. The Psalms, in particular, have been the prayer book of God's people for thousands of years. One such prayer is found in Psalm 39:4, "Lord, make me to know my end, and the measure of my days that I may know how frail I am." These prayers are literary masterpieces which are bold, daring, poetic, and rich in meaning.

The great prayer tradition did not stop in the Bible. When we open the treasure chest of church history, we find that it is full of wonderful awe-inspiring prayers that have been recorded and passed on to inspire future generations. The prayers of great men such as St. Augustine, Martin Luther, Thomas Cranmer, John Wesley, and others have laid the foundation for the devotional language of Western civilization. Their prayers can help us recover the power and meaning of the spoken word in our daily prayer lives.

The saints have left the church and the world a rich heritage and legacy by leaving us their lives and their prayers. They remind us how the Lord can do extraordinary things through ordinary people who pray. The history of the church is a treasure chest full of wisdom and gems that are free for the taking. Their prayers belong to the church; they belong to you and to me. The prayers of the saints are our prayers.

In this chapter, you will find a collection of Christian prayers which have been gathered from saints who have lived throughout the ages which will inspire and encourage your faith. Although these prayers are not directly from the Book of Common Prayer, they are timeless and applicable to our time. They stand in the common prayer tradition, which belongs to us all. As you pray these prayers, you will be drawn into the communion of the saints and reminded of the unique connection that we share with those who have gone before us.

Prayers of the Saints

Prayer of St. Clement of Rome, 1st Century

The peace of our Lord Jesus Christ be with you and with all men in all places who have been called by God and through Him, through whom be glory. *Amen.*

Prayer of St. Polycarp, 69-155

May God the Father, and the Eternal High Priest Jesus Christ, build us up in faith and truth and love, and grant to us our portion among the saints with all those who believe on our Lord Jesus Christ. We pray for all saints, for kings and rulers, for the enemies of the Cross of Christ, and for ourselves we pray that our fruit may abound and we may be made perfect in Christ Jesus our Lord. *Amen.*

Prayer of St. Thomas A Kempis, 1380-1470

Lord, You know what is best; let this be done or that be done as You please. Give what You will, as much as You will, when You will. Do with me as You know best, as will most please You, and will be for Your greater honor. Place me where You will and deal with me freely in all things. I am in Your hand; turn me about whichever way You will. Behold, I am Your servant, ready to obey in all things. Not for myself do I desire to live, but for You - would that I could do this worthily and perfectly! *Amen.*

Prayer of St Ignatius Loyola, 1491-1556

Soul of Christ, sanctify me. Body of Christ, save me. Blood of Christ, inebriate me. Water from the side of Christ, wash me. Passion of Christ, strengthen me. O good Jesus, hear me. Within thy sacred wounds hide me. From the wicked enemy defend me. In the hour of my death call me And bid me come to thee that with thy saints I may praise thee forever and ever. *Amen.*

Prayer of St. Irenaeus, 130-202

O Lamb of God, who takes away the sin of the world, look upon us and have mercy upon us; you who are yourself both victim and Priest, yourself both Reward and Redeemer, keep safe from all evil those whom thou hast redeemed, O Savior of the world. *Amen.*

Prayer of St. Chrysostom, 347-407

Almighty God, who has given us at this time with one accord to make our common prayer to you; and does promise that when two or three are gathered together in your Name you will grant their request: fulfill now, O Lord, the desires and petitions of your servants, as may be most expedient for them; granting us in this world knowledge of thy truth; and in the world to come life everlasting. *Amen.*

Prayer of St. Augustine, 354-430

Breathe in me, O Holy Spirit, that my thoughts may all be holy. Act in me, O Holy Spirit, that my work, too, may be holy. Draw my heart, O Holy Spirit, that I love but what is holy. Strengthen me, O Holy Spirit, to defend all that is holy. Guard me, then, O Holy Spirit, that I always may be holy. *Amen.*

Prayer of St. Dionysius, 3rd Century

God the Father, source of everything Divine, You are good surpassing everything good and just surpassing everything just. In You is tranquility, as well as peace and harmony. Heal our divisions and restore us to the unity of love, which is similar to Your Divine nature. Let the bond of love and the ties of Divine affection make us one in the Spirit by your peace which renders everything peaceful. We ask this through the grace, mercy, and compassion of Your only Son, our Lord Jesus Christ. *Amen.*

Prayer of St. Anselm 1033-1109

Lord, because you have made me, I owe you the whole of my love; because you have redeemed me, I owe you the whole of myself; because you have promised so much, I owe you my whole being. Moreover, I owe you as much more love than myself as you are greater than I, for whom you gave yourself and to whom you promised yourself. I pray you, Lord, make me taste by love what I taste by knowledge; let me know by love what I know by understanding. I owe you more than my whole self, but I have no more, and by myself I cannot render the whole of it to you. Draw me to you, Lord, in the fullness of your love. I am wholly yours by creation; make me all yours, too, in love. *Amen.*

Prayer of St. Francis, 1181-1226

Lord, make me an instrument of your peace. Where there is hatred, let me sow love; where there is injury,pardon; where there is doubt, faith; where there is despair, hope; where there is darkness, light; and where there is sadness, joy. O Divine Master, grant that I may not so much seek to be consoled as to console; to be understood as to understand; to be loved as to love. For it is in giving that we receive; it is in pardoning that we are pardoned; and it is in dying that we are born to eternal life. *Amen.*

Prayer of St. Patrick, 387-493

May the strength of God pilot me, the power of God uphold me, the wisdom of God guide me. May the eye of God look before me, the ear of God hear me, the Word of God speak for me. May the hand of God protect me, the way of God lie before me, the shield of God defend me, the host of God save me. May Christ shield me today. Christ with me, Christ before me, Christ behind me, Christ in me, Christ beneath me, Christ above me, Christ on my right, Christ on my left, Christ when I lie down, Christ when I sit, Christ when I stand, Christ in the heart of everyone who thinks of me, Christ in the mouth of everyone who speaks of me, Christ in every eye that sees me, Christ in every ear that hears me. *Amen.*

St. Aidan, Died 651

Leave me alone with God as much as may be. As the tide draws the waters close in upon the shore, Make me an island, set apart, alone with you, God, holy to you. Then with the turning of the tide prepare me to carry your presence to the busy world beyond, the world that rushes in on me till the waters come again and fold me back to you. *Amen.*

Prayer of St. Thomas Aquinas, 1225-1274

Grant me, O Lord my God, a mind to know you, a heart to seek you, wisdom to find you, conduct pleasing to you, faithful perseverance in waiting for you, and a hope of finally embracing you. *Amen.*

Prayer of St. Ignatius, 1491-1556

Take, O Lord, and receive all my liberty, my memory, my understanding, and my whole will. You have given me all that I am and all that I possess: I surrender it all to you that you may dispose of it according to your will. Give me only your love and your grace; with these I will be rich enough, and will have no more to desire. Glory be to the Father, and to the Son, and to the Holy Spirit. As it was in the beginning, is now, and ever shall be, world without end. *Amen.*

Prayer of St. Catherine of Siena, 1347-1380

O eternal Trinity, with the light of understanding I have tasted and seen the depths of your mystery and the beauty of your creation. In seeing myself in you, I have seen that I will become like you. O eternal Father, from your power and your wisdom clearly you have given to me a share of that wisdom which belongs to Thine Only-begotten Son. And truly have the Holy Spirit, who proceeds from you,

Father and Son, given to me the desire to love you. O
eternal Trinity, you are my maker and I am your creation.
Illuminated by you, I have learned that you have made me
a new creation through the blood of your Only-begotten
Son because you are captivated by love at the beauty of
your creation. *Amen.*

Prayer of St. Augustine, 354-430

Look upon us, O Lord, and let all the darkness of our souls
vanish before the beams of your brightness. Fill us with
holy love, and open to us the treasures of thy wisdom. All
our desire is known unto you, therefore perfect what you
have begun, and what your Spirit has awakened us to ask
in prayer. We seek your face, turn your face unto us and
show us your glory. Then shall our longing be satisfied,
and our peace shall be perfect. *Amen.*

Prayer of Clement of Rome, 1st Century

We beseech you, Master, to be our helper and protector.
Save the afflicted among us; have mercy on the lowly; raise
up the fallen; appear to the needy; heal the ungodly;
restore the wanderers of thy people; feed the hungry;
ransom our prisoners; raise up the sick; comfort the faint-
hearted. *Amen.*

Prayer of St. Ambrose of Milan, 339-397

O Lord, who hast mercy upon all, take away from me my sins, and mercifully kindle in me the fire of thy Holy Spirit. Take away from me the heart of stone, and give me a heart of flesh, a heart to love and adore you, a heart to delight in you, to follow and to enjoy you, for Christ's sake. *Amen.*

Old Celtic Prayer

Deep peace of the running wave to you, Deep peace of the flowing air to you, Deep peace of the quiet earth to you, Deep peace of the shining stars to you, Deep peace of the Son of Peace to you, for ever. *Amen.*

Prayer of St. Jerome, 342-420

O good shepherd, seek me out, and bring me home to your fold again. Deal favorably with me according to thy good pleasure, till I may dwell in your house all the days of my life, and praise you forever and ever with them that are there. *Amen.*

St. Columba, 521-597

Alone with none but you, my God, I journey on my way. What need I fear, when you are near O king of night and day? More safe am I within your hand Than if a host did round me stand. *Amen.*

Prayer of St. Jerome, 342-420

Lord, you have given us your Word for a light to shine upon our path; grant us so to meditate on that Word, and to follow its teaching, that we may find in it the light that shines more and more until the perfect day; through Jesus Christ our Lord. *Amen.*

Prayer of St. Ephrem of Syria, 306 – 373

O Lord of my life, take away from me the spirit of laziness, faint-heartedness, lust for power and idle talk. Instead grant me, your servant, the spirit of purity, humility, patience and love. Yes, O Lord and King! Grant me to see my own sins and faults and not to judge my neighbor, for you are truly blessed forever. *Amen.*

Prayer of St. Clare of Assisi, 1194-1253

Place your mind before the mirror of eternity! Place your soul in the brilliance of glory! Place your heart in the figure of the divine substance! And transform your whole being into the image of the Godhead Itself through contemplation! So that you too may feel what His friends feel as they taste the hidden sweetness which God Himself has reserved from the beginning for those who love Him. *Amen.*

Prayer of St. John Chrysostom, 347-407

Almighty God, you have given us grace at this time with one accord to make our common supplication to you; and you have promised through your well-beloved Son that when two or three are gathered together in his Name you will be in the midst of them: Fulfill now, O Lord, our desires and petitions as may be best for us; granting us in this world knowledge of your truth, and in the age to come life everlasting. *Amen.*

Prayer of St. Alcuin 735-804

Eternal Light, shine into our hearts; Eternal Goodness, deliver us from evil; Eternal Power, be our support; Eternal Wisdom, scatter the darkness of our ignorance: That we may seek Your face with all our heart and mind and soul and strength. *Amen.*

Prayer of Lancelot Andrewes 1555-1600

Be all to all. We bring before You, O God: the cries of the weary, the pains of the distressed, the tears of the tragedies of life, the anxious hours of the insecure, the restlessness of the refugees, the hunger of the oppressed. Dear God, be

near to each. Helper of the helpless, Hope of the homeless,
The Strength of those tossed with tempests, The Haven of
those who sail: Be all to all. Be within us, to strengthen us;
without us, to keep us; above us, to inspire us; beneath us,
to uphold us; before us, to direct us; behind us , to propel
us; around us, to sustain us. Be all to all in present need.
Amen.

Prayer of St. Benedict 480-547

Gracious and holy Father, give me wisdom to perceive
you, intelligence to fathom you, patience to wait for you,
eyes to behold you, a heart to meditate upon you, and a
life to proclaim you, through the power of the Spirit of
Jesus Christ our Lord. *Amen.*

Prayer of St. Caedman 658-680

Now let me praise the keeper of Heaven's kingdom, the
might of the Creator, and his thought, the work of the
Father of glory, how each of wonders the Eternal Lord
established in the beginning. He first created for the sons
of men Heaven as a roof, the holy Creator, then Middle-
earth the keeper of mankind, the Eternal Lord, afterwards
made, the earth for men, the Almighty Lord. *Amen.*

Prayer of St. Bernard of Clairvaux 1090 – 1153

Jesus, the very thought of you with sweetness fills the breast; But sweeter far your face to see, And in your presence rest. Nor voice can sing, nor heart can frame, Nor can the memory find a sweeter sound than your blessed Name, O Savior of mankind! O hope of every contrite heart, O joy of all the meek, To those who fall, how kind you are! How good to those who seek! O Jesus, light of all below, fount of living fire, surpassing all the joys we know, and all we can desire. Abide with us, and let your light shine, Lord, on every heart; Dispel the darkness of our night; And joy to all impart. *Amen.*

Chapter 6

FOR EVERYTHING THERE IS A SEASON
Praying Through the Church Year

"The church calendar aims at nothing less than to change the way we experience time and perceive reality." -Mark Galli

Every year, my family and I look forward to the different seasons. As I write this, my family is getting ready for Christmas. We have begun to develop our own family traditions, like getting our Christmas tree, baking cookies, and reading the Christmas story together. Each season brings its own unique rhythm, weather, traditions, and memories. Spring, summer, fall, and winter can be powerful reminders of the seasons and rhythms of the spiritual life. The Christian life has different seasons just as the seasons of nature. Each of these seasons remind us of the multidimensional nature of discipleship.

The Book of Common Prayer revolves around the seasons of the Church Year. The early church began to remember the various themes of the gospel of Jesus Christ by celebrating different seasons of the Christian year. By the fourth century, churches in the Holy Land began to develop liturgies to mark the days of Holy Week and

Easter at holy sites to commemorate the life and death of Jesus. Pilgrims began to travel to Jerusalem to participate in these ceremonies and eventually brought the practices back with them to their countries of origin. Today, many different Christian traditions continue to place an important role on remembering the seasons of the Christian year.

The Church Year involves an annual cycle of seasons including Advent, Epiphany, Lent, Easter, Pentecost, and Ordinary. Each season has its own unique set of prayers and themes which center on the gospel of Jesus Christ and prepare us for our journey of faith. A quick overview of the seasons of the church calendar and their meanings follows:

The season of Advent marks the beginning of the Church Year for Christians all over the world. It begins on the fourth Sunday before Christmas Day, which is the Sunday nearest November 30, and ends on Christmas Eve (Dec 24). During Advent, we prepare our hearts for the mystery of the incarnation by focusing on on the Virgin Birth and the faith of the virgin Mary, the shepherds, and the wise men.

The season following Christmas is Epiphany, in which the church proclaims Jesus to the world as Son of God, Lord, and King. Many churches remember the coming of the wise men bringing gifts to the Christ child, whereby they reveal Jesus to the world as Lord and King. This season places a strong emphasis on the human nature of Christ. Epiphany means "manifestation," "appearance," or "vision of God."

At Lent, we remember Christ's temptation, suffering, and death. During Easter, we celebrate the glorious resurrection of Christ. Lent is a forty day period beginning on Ash Wednesday that concludes the day before Easter. The climax of Lent is Holy Week, which is the week immediately preceding Easter or Resurrection Sunday. It is observed in many Christian churches as a time to commemorate and enact the last week of Jesus' life, his suffering (Passion), and his death, through various observances and services of worship.

The Easter season is the fifty days from Resurrection Sunday to Pentecost Sunday. Easter season celebrates the fact that "Christ is Risen!" It recognizes God's ongoing work of establishing new creation through the resurrection of Jesus Christ. It also celebrates the hope of that work being culminated in a new heaven and a new earth.

Literally meaning "fifty days after," the day of Pentecost falls fifty days after Easter. At Pentecost, we celebrate the coming of the Holy Spirit into our lives and the church. The season is used to celebrate the reality that God, through the power of His Holy Spirit, continues to work in, through, and among His people.

The final season is commonly referred to as "Ordinary Time." The season's name comes, not from ordinary, but the word "ordinal," which means counted time. The time, beginning on the first Sunday after

Pentecost, is used to focus on specific themes of interest or importance to a local church.

Collects of the Church

As the name suggests, the Book of Common Prayer is a book full of prayers for special seasons, days of the week, and prayers for families. Many of the prayers are called Collects and date back to the sixth century. A "Collect" is a prayer with a fixed form (address, petition, and conclusion) that is meant to be prayed together collectively. Sometimes they are prayed aloud with one voice by the congregation, and sometimes they are prayed quietly together in daily devotions. Even when we pray them privately, we are joining our hearts and minds with others, who are praying the same prayer.

These prayers are not a substitute for personal or private prayer; rather, they can help enhance and deepen our personal prayer life. Author and theologian N.T. Wright said, "I love the weekly Collects in the Book of Common Prayer... Again and again they outshine, in their elegant but profound synthesis, more recent attempts to capture Christian truth and turn it into prayer." When we pray these prayers, we connect to our Christian roots and stand with the great cloud of witnesses who have gone before us in the faith, as well as with millions of believers living today who are praying the same prayers. Here is a selection of collect prayers from the Book of Common Prayer that follows the Church Year. As you pray the collect for each week, let these prayers guide you on your spiritual journey throughout the Christian Year.

The Collects of the Church Year

First Sunday of Advent

Almighty God, give us grace to cast away the works of darkness, and put on the armor of light, now in the time of this mortal life in which your Son Jesus Christ came to visit us in great humility; that in the last day, when he shall come again in his glorious majesty to judge both the living and the dead, we may rise to the life immortal; through him who lives and reigns with you and the Holy Spirit, one God, now and for ever. *Amen.*

Second Sunday of Advent

Merciful God, who sent your messengers the prophets to preach repentance and prepare the way for our salvation: Give us grace to heed their warnings and forsake our sins, that we may greet with joy the coming of Jesus Christ our Redeemer; who lives and reigns with you and the Holy Spirit, one God, now and for ever. *Amen.*

Third Sunday of Advent

Stir up your power, O Lord, and with great might come among us; and, because we are sorely hindered by our sins, let your bountiful grace and mercy speedily help and deliver us; through Jesus Christ our Lord, to whom, with you and the Holy Spirit, be honor and glory, now and for ever. *Amen.*

Fourth Sunday of Advent

Purify our conscience, Almighty God, by your daily visitation, that your Son Jesus Christ, at his coming, may find in us a mansion prepared for himself; who lives and reigns with you, in the unity of the Holy Spirit, one God, now and for ever. *Amen.*

The Nativity of Our Lord: Christmas Day   *December 25*

O God, you make us glad by the yearly festival of the birth of your only Son Jesus Christ: Grant that we, who joyfully receive him as our Redeemer, may with sure confidence behold him when he comes to be our Judge; who lives and reigns with you and the Holy Spirit, one God, now and for ever. *Amen.*

or this

O God, you have caused this holy night to shine with the brightness of the true Light: Grant that we, who have known the mystery of that Light on earth, may also enjoy him perfectly in heaven; where with you and the Holy Spirit he lives and reigns, one God, in glory everlasting. *Amen.*

First Sunday after Christmas Day

Almighty God, you have poured upon us the new light of your incarnate Word: Grant that this light, enkindled in our hearts, may shine forth in our lives; through Jesus Christ our Lord, who lives and reigns with you, in the unity of the Holy Spirit, one God, now and for ever. *Amen.*

The Holy Name   *January 1*

Eternal Father, you gave to your incarnate Son the holy name of Jesus to be the sign of our salvation: Plant in every heart, we pray, the love of him who is the Savior of the world, our Lord Jesus Christ; who lives and reigns with you and the Holy Spirit, one God, in glory everlasting. *Amen.*

Second Sunday after Christmas Day

O God, who wonderfully created, and yet more wonderfully restored, the dignity of human nature: Grant that we may share the divine life of him who humbled himself to share our humanity, you Son Jesus Christ; who lives and reigns with you, in the unity of the Holy Spirit, one God, for ever and ever. *Amen.*

The Epiphany   *January 6*

O God, by the leading of a star you manifested your only Son to the Peoples of the earth: Lead us, who know you now by faith, to your presence, where we may see your glory face to face; through Jesus Christ our Lord, who lives and reigns with you and the Holy Spirit, one God, now and for ever.
Amen.

First Sunday after the Epiphany: The Baptism of our Lord

Father in heaven, who at the baptism of Jesus in the River Jordan proclaimed him your beloved Son and anointed him with the Holy Spirit: Grant that all who are baptized into his Name may keep the covenant they have made, and boldly confess him as Lord and Savior; who with you and the Holy Spirit lives and reigns, one God, in glory everlasting. *Amen.*

Second Sunday after the Epiphany

Almighty God, whose Son our Savior Jesus Christ is the light of the world: Grant that your people, illumined by your Word and Sacraments, may shine with the radiance of Christ's glory, that he may be known, worshiped, and obeyed to the ends of the earth; through Jesus Christ our Lord, who with you and the Holy Spirit lives and reigns, one God, now and for ever. *Amen.*

Third Sunday after the Epiphany

Give us grace, O Lord, to answer readily the call of our Savior Jesus Christ and proclaim to all people the Good News of his salvation, that we and the whole world may perceive the glory of his marvelous works; who lives and reigns with you and the Holy Spirit, one God, for ever and ever. *Amen.*

Fourth Sunday after the Epiphany

Almighty and everlasting God, you govern all things both in heaven and on earth: Mercifully hear the supplications of your people, and in our time grant us your peace; through Jesus Christ our Lord, who lives and reigns with you and the Holy Spirit, one God, for ever and ever. *Amen.*

Fifth Sunday after the Epiphany

Set us free, O God, from the bondage of our sins, and give us the liberty of that abundant life which you have made known to us in your Son our Savior Jesus Christ; who lives and reigns with you, in the unity of the Holy Spirit, one God, now and for ever. *Amen.*

Sixth Sunday after the Epiphany

O God, the strength of all who put their trust in you: Mercifully accept our prayers; and because in our weakness we can do nothing good without you, give us the help of your grace, that in keeping your commandments we may please you both in will and deed; through Jesus Christ our Lord, who lives and reigns with you and the Holy Spirit, one God, for ever and ever. *Amen.*

Seventh Sunday after the Epiphany

O Lord, you have taught us that without love whatever we do is worth nothing; Send your Holy Spirit and pour into our hearts your greatest gift, which is love, the true bond of peace and of all virtue, without which whoever lives is accounted dead before you. Grant this for the sake of your only Son Jesus Christ, who lives and reigns with you and the Holy Spirit, one God, now and for ever. *Amen.*

Eighth Sunday after the Epiphany

Most loving Father, whose will it is for us to give thanks
for all things, to fear nothing but the loss of you, and to
cast all our care on you who care for us: Preserve us from
faithless fears and worldly anxieties, that no clouds of this
mortal life may hide from us the light of that love which is
immortal, and which you have manifested to us in your
Son Jesus Christ our Lord; who lives and reigns with you,
in the unity of the Holy Spirit, one God, now and for ever.
Amen.

Last Sunday after the Epiphany

O God, who before the passion of your only-begotten Son
revealed his glory upon the holy mountain: Grant to us
that we, beholding by faith the light of his countenance,
may be strengthened to bear our cross, and be changed
into his likeness from glory to glory; through Jesus Christ
our Lord, who lives and reigns with you and the Holy
Spirit, one God, for ever and ever. *Amen.*

Ash Wednesday

Almighty and everlasting God, you hate nothing you have
made and forgive the sins of all who are penitent: Create
and make in us new and contrite hearts, that we, worthily
lamenting our sins and acknowledging our wretchedness,

may obtain of you, the God of all mercy, perfect remission
and forgiveness; through Jesus Christ our Lord, who lives
and reigns with you and the Holy Spirit, one God, for ever
and ever. *Amen.*

First Sunday in Lent

Almighty God, whose blessed Son was led by the Spirit to
be tempted by Satan; Come quickly to help us who are
assaulted by many temptations; and, as you know the
weaknesses of each of us, let each one find you mighty to
save; through Jesus Christ your Son our Lord, who lives
and reigns with you and the Holy Spirit, one God, now
and for ever. *Amen.*

Second Sunday in Lent

O God, whose glory it is always to have mercy: Be
gracious to all who have gone astray from your ways, and
bring them again with penitent hearts and steadfast faith
to embrace and hold fast the unchangeable truth of your
Word, Jesus Christ your Son; who with you and the Holy
Spirit lives and reigns, one God, for ever and ever. *Amen.*

Third Sunday in Lent

Almighty God, you know that we have no power in
ourselves to help ourselves: Keep us both outwardly in our

bodies and inwardly in our souls, that we may be defended from all adversities which may happen to the body, and from all evil thoughts which may assault and hurt the soul; through Jesus Christ our Lord, who lives and reigns with you and the Holy Spirit, one God, for ever and ever. *Amen.*

Fourth Sunday in Lent

Gracious Father, whose blessed Son Jesus Christ came down from heaven to be the true bread which gives life to the world: Evermore give us this bread, that he may live in us, and we in him; who lives and reigns with you and the Holy Spirit, one God, now and for ever. *Amen.*

Fifth Sunday in Lent

Almighty God, you alone can bring into order the unruly wills and affections of sinners: Grant your people grace to love what you command and desire what you promise; that, among the swift and varied changes of the world, our hearts may surely there be fixed where true joys are to be found; through Jesus Christ our Lord, who lives and reigns with you and the Holy Spirit, one God, now and for ever. *Amen.*

Sunday of the Passion: Palm Sunday

Almighty and everliving God, in your tender love for the human race you sent your Son our Savior Jesus Christ to take upon him our nature, and to suffer death upon the cross, giving us the example of his great humility: Mercifully grant that we may walk in the way of his suffering, and also share in his resurrection; through Jesus Christ our Lord, who lives and reigns with you and the Holy Spirit, one God, for ever and ever. *Amen.*

Monday in Holy Week

Almighty God, whose dear Son went not up to joy but first he suffered pain, and entered not into glory before he was crucified: Mercifully grant that we, walking in the way of the cross, may find it none other that the way of life and peace; through Jesus Christ your Son our Lord, who lives and reigns with you and the Holy Spirit, one God, for ever and ever. *Amen.*

Tuesday in Holy Week

O God, by the passion of your blessed Son you made an instrument of shameful death to be for us the means of life: Grant us so to glory in the cross of Christ, that we may gladly suffer shame and loss for the sake of your Son our

Savior Jesus Christ; who lives and reigns with you and the Holy Spirit, one God, for ever and ever. *Amen.*

Wednesday in Holy Week

Lord God, whose blessed Son our Savior gave his body to be whipped and his face to be spit upon: Give us grace to accept joyfully the sufferings of the present time, confident of the glory that shall be revealed; through Jesus Christ your Son our Lord, who lives and reigns with you and the Holy Spirit, one God, for ever and ever. *Amen.*

Maundy Thursday

Almighty Father, whose dear Son, on the night before he suffered, instituted the Sacrament of his Body and Blood: Mercifully grant that we may receive it thankfully in remembrance of Jesus Christ our Lord, who in these holy mysteries gives us a pledge of eternal life; and who now lives and reigns with you and the Holy Spirit, one God, for ever and ever. *Amen.*

Good Friday

Almighty God, we pray you graciously to behold this your family, for whom our Lord Jesus Christ was willing to be betrayed, and given into the hands of sinners, and to suffer

death upon the cross; who now lives and reigns with you
and the Holy Spirit, one God, for ever and ever. *Amen.*

Holy Saturday

O God, Creator of heaven and earth: Grant that, as the
crucified body of your dear Son was laid in the tomb and
rested on this holy Sabbath, so we may await with him the
coming of the third day, and rise with him to newness of
life; who now lives and reigns with you and the Holy
Spirit, one God, for ever and ever. *Amen.*

Easter Day

O God, who for our redemption gave your only-begotten
Son to the death of the cross, and by his glorious
resurrection delivered us from the power of our enemy:
Grant us so to die daily to sin, that we may evermore live
with him in the joy of his resurrection; through Jesus
Christ your Son our Lord, who lives and reigns with you
and the Holy Spirit, one God, now and for ever. *Amen.*

or this

O God, who made this most holy night to shine with the
glory of the Lord's resurrection: Stir up in your Church
that Spirit of adoption which is given to us in Baptism, that
we, being renewed both in body and mind, may worship

you in sincerity and truth; through Jesus Christ our Lord, who lives and reigns with you, in the unity of the Holy Spirit, one God, now and for ever. *Amen.*

or this

Almighty God, who through your only-begotten Son Jesus Christ overcame death and opened to us the gate of everlasting life: Grant that we, who celebrate with joy the day of the Lord's resurrection, may be raised from the death of sin by your life-giving Spirit; through Jesus Christ our Lord, who lives and reigns with you and the Holy Spirit, one God, now and for ever. *Amen.*

Monday in Easter Week

Grant, we pray, Almighty God, that we who celebrate with awe the Paschal feast may be found worthy to attain to everlasting joys; through Jesus Christ our Lord, who lives and reigns with you and the Holy Spirit, one God, now and for ever. *Amen.*

Tuesday in Easter Week

O God, who by the glorious resurrection of your Son Jesus Christ destroyed death and brought life and immortality to light: Grant that we, who have been raised with him, may abide in his presence and rejoice in the hope of eternal glory; through Jesus Christ our Lord, to whom, with you and the Holy Spirit, be dominion and praise for ever and ever. *Amen.*

Wednesday in Easter Week

O God, whose blessed Son made himself known to his disciples in the breaking of bread: Open the eyes of our faith, that we may behold him in all his redeeming work; who lives and reigns with you, in the unity of the Holy Spirit, one God, now and for ever. *Amen.*

Preface of Easter

Thursday in Easter Week

Almighty and everlasting God, who in the Paschal mystery established the new covenant of reconciliation: Grant that all who have been reborn into the fellowship of Christ's Body may show forth in their lives what they profess by their faith; through Jesus Christ our Lord, who lives and reigns with you and the Holy Spirit, one God, for ever and ever. *Amen.*

Friday in Easter Week

Almighty Father, who gave your only Son to die for our sins and to rise for our justification: Give us grace so to put away the leaven of malice and wickedness, that we may always serve you in pureness of living and truth; through Jesus Christ your Son our Lord, who lives and reigns with you and the Holy Spirit, one God, now and for ever. *Amen.*

Saturday in Easter Week

We thank you, heavenly Father, that you have delivered us from the dominion of sin and death and brought us into the kingdom of your Son; and we pray that, as by his death he has recalled us to life, so by his love he may raise us to eternal joys; who lives and reigns with you, in the unity of the Holy Spirit, one God, now and forever. *Amen.*

Second Sunday of Easter

Almighty and everlasting God, who in the Paschal mystery established the new covenant of reconciliation: Grant that all who have been reborn into the fellowship of Christ's Body may show forth in their lives what they profess by their faith; through Jesus Christ our Lord, who lives and reigns with you and the Holy Spirit, one God, for ever and ever. *Amen.*

Third Sunday of Easter

O God, whose blessed Son made himself known to his disciples in the breaking of bread: Open the eyes of our faith, that we may behold him in all his redeeming work; who lives and reigns with you, in the unity of the Holy Spirit, one God, now and for ever. *Amen.*

Fourth Sunday of Easter

O God, whose Son Jesus is the good shepherd of your people; Grant that when we hear his voice we may know him who calls us each by name, and follow where he leads; who, with you and the Holy Spirit, lives and reigns, one God, for ever and ever. *Amen.*

Fifth Sunday of Easter

Almighty god, whom truly to know is everlasting life: Grant us so perfectly to know your Son Jesus Christ to be the way, the truth, and the life, that we may steadfastly follow his steps in the way that leads to eternal life; through Jesus Christ your Son our Lord, who lives and reigns with you, in the unity of the Holy Spirit, one God, for ever and ever. *Amen.*

Sixth Sunday of Easter

O God, you have prepared for those who love you such good things as surpass our understanding: Pour into our hearts such love towards you, that we, loving you in all things and above all things, may obtain your promises, which exceed all that we can desire; through Jesus Christ our Lord, who lives and reigns with you and the Holy Spirit, one God, for ever and ever. *Amen.*

Ascension Day

Almighty God, whose blessed Son our Savior Jesus Christ ascended far above all heavens that he might fill all things: Mercifully give us faith to perceive that, according to his promise, he abides with his Church on earth, even to the end of the ages; through Jesus Christ our Lord, who lives and reigns with you and the Holy Spirit, one God, in glory everlasting. *Amen.*

or this

Grant, we pray, Almighty God, that as we believe your only-begotten Son our Lord Jesus Christ to have ascended into heaven, so we may also in heart and mind there ascend, and with him continually dwell; who lives and reigns with you and the Holy Spirit, one God, for ever and ever. *Amen.*

Seventh Sunday of Easter: The Sunday after Ascension Day

O God, the King of glory, you have exalted your only Son Jesus Christ with great triumph to your kingdom in heaven: Do not leave us comfortless, but send us your Holy Spirit to strengthen us, and exalt us to that place where our Savior Christ has gone before; who lives and reigns with you and the Holy Spirit, one God, in glory everlasting. *Amen.*

The Day of Pentecost: Whitsunday

Almighty God, on this day you opened the way of eternal life to every race and nation by the promised gift of your Holy Spirit: Shed abroad this gift throughout the world by the preaching of the Gospel, that it may reach to the ends of the earth; through Jesus Christ our Lord, who lives and reigns with you, in the unity of the Holy Spirit, one God, for ever and ever. *Amen.*

or this

O God, who on this day taught the hearts of your faithful people by sending to them the light of your Holy Spirit: Grant us by the same Spirit to have a right judgment in all things, and evermore to rejoice in his holy comfort; through Jesus Christ your Son our Lord, who lives and reigns with you, in the unity of the Holy Spirit, one God, for ever and ever. *Amen.*

First Sunday after Pentecost: Trinity Sunday

Almighty and everlasting God, you have given to us your servants grace, by the confession of a true faith, to acknowledge the glory of the eternal Trinity, and in the power of your divine Majesty to worship the Unity: Keep us steadfast in this faith and worship, and bring us at last to see you in your one and eternal glory, O Father; who with the Son and the Holy Spirit live and reign, one God, for ever and ever. *Amen.*

The Season after Pentecost

Proper 1 *Week of the Sunday closest to May 11*

Remember, O Lord, what you have wrought in us and not what we deserve; and, as you have called us to your service, make us worthy of our calling; through Jesus Christ our Lord, who lives and reigns with you and the Holy Spirit, one God, now and for ever. *Amen.*

Proper 2 *Week of the Sunday closest to May 18*

Almighty and merciful God, in your goodness keep us, we pray, from all things that may hurt us, that we, being ready both in mind and body, may accomplish with free hearts those things which belong to your purpose; through Jesus

Christ our Lord, who lives and reigns with you and the Holy Spirit, one God, now and for ever. *Amen.*

Proper 3   *The Sunday closest to May 25*

Grant, O Lord, that the course of this world may be peaceably governed by your providence; and that your Church may joyfully serve you in confidence and serenity; through Jesus Christ our Lord, who lives and reigns with you and the Holy Spirit, one God, for ever and ever. *Amen.*

Proper 4   *The Sunday closest to June 1*

O God, your never-failing providence sets in order all things both in heaven and earth: Put away from us, we entreat you, all hurtful things, and give us those things which are profitable for us; through Jesus Christ our Lord, who lives and reigns with you and the Holy Spirit, one God, for ever and ever. *Amen.*

Proper 5   *The Sunday closest to June 8*

O God, from whom all good proceeds: Grant that by your inspiration we may think those things that are right, and by your merciful guiding may do them; through Jesus Christ our Lord, who lives and reigns with you and the Holy Spirit, one God, for ever and ever. *Amen.*

Proper 6   The Sunday closest to June 15

Keep, O Lord, your household the Church in your
steadfast faith and love, that through your grace we may
proclaim your truth with boldness, and minister your
justice with compassion; for the sake of our Savior Jesus
Christ, who lives and reigns with you and the Holy Spirit,
one God, now and for ever. *Amen.*

Proper 7   *The Sunday closest to June 22*

O Lord, make us have perpetual love and reverence for
your holy Name, for you never fail to help and govern
those whom you have set upon the sure foundation of
your loving-kindness; through Jesus Christ our Lord, who
lives and reigns with you and the Holy Spirit, one God, for
ever and ever. *Amen.*

Proper 8   *The Sunday closest to June 29*

Almighty God, you have built your Church upon the
foundation of the apostles and prophets, Jesus Christ
himself being the chief cornerstone: Grant us so to be
joined together in unity of spirit by their teaching, that we
may be made a holy temple acceptable to you; through
Jesus Christ our Lord, who lives and reigns with you and
the Holy Spirit, one God, for ever and ever. *Amen.*

Proper 9   *The Sunday closest to July 6*

O God, you have taught us to keep all your
commandments by loving you and our neighbor: Grant us
the grace of your Holy Spirit, that we may be devoted to
your with our whole heart, and united to one another with
pure affection; through Jesus Christ our Lord, who lives
and reigns with you and the Holy Spirit, one God, for ever
and ever. *Amen.*

Proper 10   *The Sunday closest to July 13*

O Lord, mercifully receive the prayers of your people who
call upon you, and grant that they may know and
understand what things they ought to do, and also may
have grace and power faithfully to accomplish them;
through Jesus Christ our Lord, who lives and reigns with
you and the Holy Spirit, one God, now and for ever. *Amen.*

Proper 11   *The Sunday closest to July 20*

Almighty God, the fountain of all wisdom, you know our
necessities before we ask and our ignorance in asking:
Have compassion on our weakness, and mercifully give us
those things which for our unworthiness we dare not, and
for our blindness we cannot ask; through the worthiness of
your Son Jesus Christ our Lord, who lives and reigns with
you and the Holy Spirit, one God, now and for ever. *Amen.*

Proper 12 *The Sunday closest to July 27*

O god, the protector of all who trust in you, without whom
nothing is strong, nothing is holy: Increase and multiply
upon us your mercy; that, with you as our ruler and guide,
we may so pass through things temporal, that we lose not
the things eternal; through Jesus Christ our Lord, who
lives and reigns with you and the Holy Spirit, one God, for
ever and ever. *Amen.*

Proper 13 *The Sunday closest to August 3*

Let your continual mercy, O Lord, cleanse and defend your
Church; and, because it cannot continue in safety without
your help, protect and govern it always by your goodness;
through Jesus Christ our Lord, who lives and reigns with
you and the Holy Spirit, one God, for ever and ever. *Amen.*

Proper 14 *The Sunday closest to August 10*

Grant to us, Lord, we pray, the spirit to think and do
always those things that are right, that we, who cannot
exist without you, may by you be enabled to live according
to your will; through Jesus Christ our Lord, who lives and
reigns with you and the Holy Spirit, one God, for ever and
ever. *Amen.*

Proper 15   *The Sunday closest to August 17*

Almighty God, you have given your only Son to be for us a sacrifice for sin, and also an example of godly life: Give us grace to receive thankfully the fruits of this redeeming work, and to follow daily in the blessed steps of his most holy life; through Jesus Christ your Son our Lord, who lives and reigns with you and the Holy Spirit, one God, now and for ever. *Amen.*

Proper 16   *The Sunday closest to August 24*

Grant, O merciful God, that your Church, being gathered together in unity by your Holy Spirit, may show forth your power among all peoples, to the glory of your Name; through Jesus Christ our Lord, who liveth and reigns with thee and the Holy Spirit, one God, world without end. *Amen.*

Proper 17   The Sunday closest to August 31

Lord of all power and might, the author and giver of all good things: Graft in our hearts the love of your Name; increase in us true religion; nourish us with all goodness; and bring forth in us the fruit of good works; through Jesus Christ our Lord, who lives and reigns with you and the Holy Spirit, one God, for ever and ever. *Amen.*

Proper 18   *The Sunday closest to September 7*

Grant us, O Lord, to trust in you with all our hearts; for, as you always resist the proud who confide in their own strength, so you never forsake those who make their boast of your mercy; through Jesus Christ our Lord, who lives and reigns with you and the Holy Spirit, one God, now and for ever. *Amen.*

Proper 19   The Sunday closest to September 14

O God, because without you we are not able to please you, mercifully grant that your Holy Spirit may in all things direct and rule our hearts; through Jesus Christ our Lord, who lives and reigns with you and the Holy Spirit, one God, now and for ever. *Amen.*

Proper 20   *The Sunday closest to September 21*

Grant us, Lord, not to be anxious about earthly things, but to love things heavenly; and even now, while we are placed among things that are passing away, to hold fast to those that shall endure; through Jesus Christ our Lord, who lives and reigns with you and the Holy Spirit, one God, for ever and ever. *Amen.*

Proper 21 *The Sunday closest to September 28*

O God, you declare your almighty power chiefly in
showing mercy and pity: Grant us the fullness of your
grace, that we, running to obtain your promises, may
become partakers of your heavenly treasure; through Jesus
Christ our Lord, who lives and reigns with you and the
Holy Spirit, one God, for ever and ever. *Amen.*

Proper 22 *The Sunday closest to October 5*

Almighty and everlasting God, you are always more ready
to hear than we to pray, and to give more than we either
desire or deserve: Pour upon us the abundance of your
mercy, forgiving us those things of which our conscience is
afraid, and giving us those good things for which we are
not worthy to ask, except through the merits and
mediation of Jesus Christ our Savior; who lives and reigns
with you and the Holy Spirit, one God, for ever and ever.
Amen.

Proper 23 *The Sunday closest to October 12*

Lord, we pray that your grace may always precede and
follow us, that we may continually be given to good
works; through Jesus Christ our Lord, who lives and reigns
with you and the Holy Spirit, one God, now and for ever.
Amen.

Proper 24 *The Sunday closest to October 19*

Almighty and everlasting God, in Christ you have revealed your glory among the nations: Preserve the works of your mercy, that your Church throughout the world may persevere with steadfast faith in the confession of your Name; through Jesus Christ our Lord, who lives and reigns with you and the Holy Spirit, one God, for ever and ever. *Amen.*

Proper 25 *The Sunday closest to October 26*

Almighty and everlasting God, increase in us the gifts of faith, hope, and charity; and, that we may obtain what you promise, make us love what you command; through Jesus Christ our Lord, who lives and reigns with you and the Holy Spirit, one God, for ever and ever. *Amen.*

Proper 26 The Sunday closest to November 2

Almighty and merciful God, it is only by your gift that your faithful people offer you true and laudable service: Grant that we may run without stumbling to obtain your heavenly promises; through Jesus Christ our Lord, who lives and reigns with you and the Holy Spirit, one God, now and for ever. *Amen.*

Proper 27   *The Sunday closest to November 9*

O God, whose blessed Son came into the world that he
might destroy the works of the devil and make us children
of God and heirs of eternal life: Grant that, having this
hope, we may purify ourselves as he is pure; that, when he
comes again with power and great glory, we may be made
like him in his eternal and glorious kingdom; where he
lives and reigns with you and the Holy Spirit, one God, for
ever and ever. *Amen.*

Proper 28   *The Sunday closest to November 16*

Blessed Lord, who caused all holy Scriptures to be written
for our learning: Grant us so to hear them, read, mark,
learn, and inwardly digest them, that we may embrace and
ever hold fast the blessed hope of everlasting life, which
you have given us in our Savior Jesus Christ; who lives
and reigns with you and the Holy Spirit, one God, for ever
and ever. *Amen.*

Proper 29   *The Sunday closest to November 23*

Almighty and everlasting God, whose will it is to restore
all things in your well-beloved Son, the King of kings and
Lord of lords: Mercifully grant that the peoples of the
earth, divided and enslaved by sin, may be freed and
brought together under his most gracious rule; who lives

and reigns with you and the Holy Spirit, one God, now
and for ever. *Amen.*

Holy Days

Saint Andrew   *November 30*

Almighty God, who gave such grace to your apostle
Andrew that he readily obeyed the call of your Son Jesus
Christ, and brought his brother with him: Give us, who are
called by your holy Word, grace to follow him without
delay, and to bring those near to us into his gracious
presence; who lives and reigns with you and the Holy
Spirit, one God, now and for ever. *Amen.*

Saint Thomas   *December 21*

Everliving God, who strengthened your apostle Thomas
with firm and certain faith in your Son's resurrection:
Grant us so perfectly and without doubt to believe in Jesus
Christ, our Lord and our God, that our faith may never be
found wanting in your sight; through him who lives and
reigns with you and the Holy Spirit, one God, now and for
ever. *Amen.*

Saint Stephen *December 26*

We give you thanks, O Lord of glory, for the example of the first martyr Stephen, who looked up to heaven and prayed for his persecutors to your Son Jesus Christ, who stands at your right hand; where he lives and reigns with you and the Holy Spirit, one God, in glory everlasting. *Amen.*

Saint John *December 27*

Shed upon your Church, O Lord, the brightness of your light, that we, being illumined by the teaching of your apostle and evangelist John, may so walk in the light of your truth, that at length we may attain to the fullness of eternal life; through Jesus Christ our Lord, who lives and reigns with you and the Holy Spirit, one God, for ever and ever. *Amen.*

The Holy Innocents *December 28*

We remember today, O God, the slaughter of the holy innocents of Bethlehem by King Herod. Receive, we pray, into the arms of your mercy all innocent victims; and by your great might frustrate the designs of evil tyrants and establish your rule of justice, love, and peace; through Jesus Christ our Lord, who lives and reigns with you, in the unity of the Holy Spirit,, one God, for ever and ever. *Amen.*

Confession of Saint Peter   *January 18*

Almighty Father, who inspired Saint Peter, first among the apostles, to confess Jesus as Messiah and Son of the living God: Keep your Church steadfast upon the rock of this faith, so that in unity and peace we may proclaim the one truth and follow the one Lord, our Savior Jesus Christ; who lives and reigns with you and the Holy Spirit, one God, now and for ever. *Amen.*

Conversion of Saint Paul   *January 25*

O God, by the preaching of your apostle Paul you have caused the light of the Gospel to shine throughout the world: Grant, we pray, that we, having his wonderful conversion in remembrance, may show ourselves thankful to you by following his holy teaching; through Jesus Christ our Lord, who lives and reigns with you, in the unity of the Holy Spirit, one God, now and for ever. *Amen.*

The Presentation   *February 2*

Almighty and everliving God, we humbly pray that, as your only-begotten Son was this day presented in the temple, so we may be presented to you with pure and clean hearts by Jesus Christ our Lord; who lives and reigns with you and the Holy Spirit, one God, now and for ever. *Amen.*

Saint Matthias   *February 24*

Almighty God, who in the place of Judas chose your
faithful servant Matthias to be numbered among the
Twelve: Grant that your Church, being delivered from false
apostles, may always be guided and governed by faithful
and true pastors; through Jesus Christ our Lord, who lives
and reigns with you, in the unity of the Holy Spirit, one
God, now and for ever. *Amen.*

Saint Joseph   *March 19*

O God, who from the family of your servant David raised
up Joseph to be the guardian of your incarnate Son and the
spouse of his virgin mother: Give us grace to imitate his
uprightness of life and his obedience to your commands;
through Jesus Christ our Lord, who lives and reigns with
you and the Holy Spirit, one God, for ever and ever. *Amen.*

The Annunciation   *March 25*

Pour your grace into our hearts, O Lord, that we who have
known the incarnation of your Son Jesus Christ,
announced by an angel to the Virgin Mary, may by his
cross and passion be brought to the glory of his
resurrection; who lives and reigns with you, in the unity of
the Holy Spirit, one God, now and for ever. *Amen.*

Saint Mark   *April 25*

Almighty God, by the hand of Mark the evangelist you
have given to your Church the Gospel of Jesus Christ the
Son of God: We thank you for this witness, and pray that
we may be firmly grounded in its truth; through Jesus
Christ our Lord, who lives and reigns with you and the
Holy Spirit, one God, for ever and ever. *Amen.*

Saint Philip and Saint James   *May 1*

Almighty God, who gave to your apostles Philip and
James grace and strength to bear witness to the truth:
Grant that we, being mindful of their victory of faith, may
glorify in life and death the Name of our Lord Jesus Christ;
who lives and reigns with you and the Holy Spirit, one
God, now and for ever. *Amen.*

The Visitation   *May 31*

Father in heaven, by your grace the virgin mother of your
incarnate Son was blessed in bearing him, but still more
blessed in keeping your word: Grant us who honor the
exaltation of her lowliness to follow the example of her
devotion to your will; through Jesus Christ our Lord,
who lives and reigns with you and the Holy Spirit, one
God, for ever and ever. *Amen.*

Saint Barnabas   *June 11*

Grant, O God, that we may follow the example of your
faithful servant Barnabas, who, seeking not his own
renown but the well-being of your Church, gave
generously of his life and substance for the relief of the
poor and the spread of the Gospel; through Jesus Christ
our Lord, who lives and reigns with you and the Holy
Spirit, one God, for ever and ever. *Amen.*

The Nativity of Saint John the Baptist   *June 24*

Almighty God, by whose providence your servant John
the Baptist was wonderfully born, and sent to prepare the
way of your Son our Savior by preaching repentance:
Make us so to follow his teaching and holy life, that we
may truly repent according to his preaching; and,
following his example, constantly speak the truth, boldly
rebuke vice, and patiently suffer for the truth's sake;
through Jesus Christ your Son our Lord, who lives and
reigns with you and the Holy Spirit, one God, for ever and
ever. *Amen.*

Saint Peter and Saint Paul   *June 29*

Almighty God, whose blessed apostles Peter and Paul
glorified you by their martyrdom: Grant that your Church,
instructed by their teaching and example, and knit

together in unity by your Spirit, may ever stand firm upon the one foundation, which is Jesus Christ our Lord; who lives and reigns with you, in the unity of the Holy Spirit, one God, now and for ever. *Amen.*

Independence Day   *July 4*

Lord God Almighty, in whose Name the founders of this country won liberty for themselves and for us, and lit the torch of freedom for nations then unborn: Grant that we and all the people of this land may have grace to maintain our liberties in righteousness and peace; through Jesus Christ our Lord, who lives and reigns with you and the Holy Spirit, one God, for ever and ever. *Amen.*

Saint Mary Magdalene   *July 22*

Almighty God, whose blessed Son restored Mary Magdalene to health of body and of mind, and called her to be a witness of his resurrection: Mercifully grant that by your grace we may be healed from all our infirmities and know you in the power of his unending life; who with you and the Holy Spirit lives and reigns, one God, now and for ever. *Amen.*

Saint James *July 25*

O gracious God, we remember before you today your
servant and apostle James, first among the Twelve to suffer
martyrdom for the Name of Jesus Christ; and we pray that
you will pour out upon the leaders of your Church that
spirit of self-denying service by which alone they may
have true authority among your people; through Jesus
Christ our Lord, who lives and reigns with you and the
Holy Spirit, one God, now and for ever. *Amen.*

The Transfiguration *August 6*

O God, who on the holy mount revealed to chosen
witnesses your well-beloved Son, wonderfully
transfigured, in raiment white and glistening: Mercifully
grant that we, being delivered from the disquietude of this
world, may by faith behold the King in his beauty; who
with you, O Father, and you, O Holy Spirit, lives and
reigns, one God, for ever and ever. *Amen.*

Saint Mary the Virgin *August 15*

O God, you have taken to yourself the blessed Virgin Mary,
mother of your incarnate Son: Grant that we, who have
been redeemed by his blood, may share with her the glory
of your eternal kingdom; through Jesus Christ our Lord,

who lives and reigns with you, in the unity of the Holy
Spirit, one God, now and for ever. *Amen.*

Saint Bartholomew   *August 24*

Almighty and everlasting God, who gave to your apostle
Bartholomew grace truly to believe and to preach your
Word: Grant that your Church may love what he believed
and preach what he taught; through Jesus Christ our Lord,
who lives and reigns with you and the Holy Spirit, one
God, for ever and ever. *Amen.*

Holy Cross Day   *September 14*

Almighty God, whose Son our Savior Jesus Christ was
lifted high upon the cross that he might draw the whole
world to himself: Mercifully grant that we, who glory in
the mystery of our redemption, may have grace to take up
our cross and follow him; who lives and reigns with you
and the Holy Spirit, one God, in glory everlasting. *Amen.*

Saint Matthew   *September 21*

We thank you, heavenly Father, for the witness of your
apostle and evangelist Matthew to the Gospel of your Son
our Savior; and we pray that, after his example, we may
with ready wills and hearts obey the calling of our Lord to
follow him; through Jesus Christ our Lord, who lives and

reigns with you and the Holy Spirit, one God, now and for ever. *Amen.*

Saint Michael and All Angels   *September 29*

Everlasting God, you have ordained and constituted in a wonderful order the ministries of angels and mortals: Mercifully grant that, as your holy angels always serve and worship you in heaven, so by your appointment they may help and defend us here on earth; through Jesus Christ our Lord, who lives and reigns with you and the Holy Spirit, one God, for ever and ever. *Amen.*

Saint Luke   *October 18*

Almighty God, who inspired your servant Luke the physician to set forth in the Gospel the love and healing power of your Son: Graciously continue in your Church this love and power to heal, to the praise and glory of your Name; through Jesus Christ our Lord, who lives and reigns with you, in the unity of the Holy Spirit, one God, now and for ever. *Amen.*

Saint James of Jerusalem   *October 23*

Grant, O God, that, following the example of your servant James the Just, brother of our Lord, your Church may give itself continually to prayer and to the reconciliation of all who are at variance and enmity; through Jesus Christ our Lord, who lives and reigns with you and the Holy Spirit, one God, now and for ever. *Amen.*

Saint Simon and Saint Jude *October 28*

O God, we thank you for the glorious company of the apostles, and especially on this day for Simon and Jude; and we pray that, as they were faithful and zealous in their mission, so we may with ardent devotion make known the love and mercy of our Lord and Savior Jesus Christ; who lives and reigns with you and the Holy Spirit, one God, for ever and ever. *Amen.*

All Saint's Day *November 1*

Almighty God, you have knit together your elect in one communion and fellowship in the mystical body of your Son Christ our Lord: Give us grace so to follow your blessed saints in all virtuous and godly living, that we may come to those ineffable joys that you have prepared for those who truly love you; through Jesus Christ our Lord, who with you and the Holy Spirit lives and reigns, one God, in glory everlasting. *Amen.*

Thanksgiving Day

Almighty and gracious Father, we give you thanks for the fruits of the earth in their season and for the labors of those who harvest them. Make us, we pray, faithful stewards of your great bounty, for the provision of our necessities and the relief of all who are in need, to the glory of your Name; through Jesus Christ our Lord, who lives and reigns with you and the Holy Spirit, one God, now and for ever. *Amen.*

Chapter 7

PASTURES OF THE SOUL
Encountering God in the Scriptures

"In the scriptures be the fat pastures of the soul." -Thomas Cranmer

Christians have the audacious belief that the Bible is not the work of mere men to be read like a novel or newspaper, but that it is actually the Word of the Living God. The Bible says, "All Scripture is given by inspiration of God" (2 Timothy 3:16, NKJV). Inspiration literally means *God-breathed*. So if you believe the Bible is actually God's inspired Word, then the implications are absolutely astounding and a whole new world of possibilities begins to open up to you.

To enter the world of the Bible, you must follow the footsteps of St. Augustine and millions of others and *"Tolle Lege*- Take up and read!" There is nothing more important or valuable than a regular systematic study of the Bible. Jesus told his disciples, "If you abide in my word, you are truly my disciples, and you will know the truth, and the truth will set you free"(John 8:31, ESV). Bible reading is absolutely essential for spiritual growth because the Scriptures shape and form us into the men and women that God has called us to be.

As we read the Bible every day, it strengthens our faith, speaks to our heart, and guides us in all of life's tough decisions. Through the pages of Scripture, God reveals His plans and purposes for our life. Anglican Bishop and author N.T. Wright says the Scriptures, "form the habits of mind and heart, of soul and body, which will slowly but surely form your character into the likeness of Jesus Christ."

Reading the Bible is not just an intellectual exercise to increase one's knowledge about God; rather, it is the place where we encounter the living God through His Word. Just as Moses encountered God in the burning bush, we also come face to face with God through the Scriptures. A. W. Tozer reminds us:

> "The Bible is not an end in itself, but a means to bring men to an intimate and satisfying knowledge of God, that they may enter into Him, that they may delight in His Presence, may taste and know the inner sweetness of the very God Himself in the core and center of their hearts."

The Scriptures introduce the reader to the Holy Spirit, and the Spirit makes them come alive as He applies the truths of the Word to the hearts of the reader.

Prayer and Bible Study

Prayer and Bible study are inseparably linked. Scripture should always be read in the context of personal prayer because prayer is the medium that brings us into contact with the same Holy Spirit who inspired the writers of the Bible. As we read the Scriptures, the Spirit applies the truths of the Word to our hearts. To hear what the Lord is saying through the Word one must encounter God through prayer. Prayer is the means that we must use to understand the Word of God. Without the assistance of the Holy Spirit in prayer, our Bible study will be in vain.

No one knew this more than Thomas Cranmer. He cherished the Word of God and sought to make it the very foundation of the Book of Common Prayer by saturating it with Scriptures from the Old and New Testament. He was a product of the Reformation and firmly believed the "Holy Scriptures containeth all things necessary to salvation." He knew the importance of daily reading the Scriptures. He said, "The people (by daily hearing of holy Scripture read in the Church) should continually profit more and more in the knowledge of God, and be the more inflamed with the love of his true religion."

The love of Scriptures were intricately connected to his understanding of common prayer. For Cranmer, Scripture and prayer go together. In fact, it could be said the two cannot be separated. Cranmer's vision for the daily office weaved together a matrix of prayer and Scripture, exposing the reader to the presence of the Living

Word. Cranmer's Collect for the second Sunday of Advent shows his love for the Scriptures:

> "Blessed Lord, who hast caused all holy Scriptures to be written for our learning; Grant that we may in such wise hear them, read, mark, learn, and inwardly digest them, that by patience, and comfort of thy holy Word, we may embrace and ever hold fast the blessed hope of everlasting life, which thou hast given us in our Saviour Jesus Christ. Amen."

Thomas Cranmer's vision for common prayer included reading Scripture daily throughout the year. In Cranmer's preface to the first English Prayer Book of 1549 he noted, "The ancient fathers... so ordered the matter, that all the whole Bible (or the greatest part thereof) should be read over once in the year." Cranmer restored the ancient practice of reading through the entire Bible in daily prayer. Bishop John Howe says:

> "In a stroke of genius, he (Thomas Cranmer) made the Church of England the greatest Bible reading church in the world. Nowhere else is the Bible read so regularly, so comprehensively, and at such length as in the public worship of the Anglican Communion."

Cranmer's greatest desire was to put the Bible and prayer in the hands of ordinary people so that their hearts and lives would be transformed by the God of the Bible. This is why Cranmer devised a Bible reading plan where everyone could hear the Scriptures daily and regularly. Here are several things that we can learn about reading the Bible from Cranmer's preface to 1549 Book of Common Prayer.

- The Bible should be read by everyone. In the spirit of the Reformation, Cranmer wanted every man, woman, boy, and girl to have access to the Word of God in their own language.
- The Bible should be read everyday. Cranmer wanted to Christians to be exposed to the Word of God daily through morning and evening prayer.
- The Bible should be read through in a year. Cranmer devised a Bible reading plan that would allow people to hear the Bible read through in a year.
- The Bible should be read privately and publicly in worship. The uniqueness of Cranmer's common prayer is that it was meant to facilitate both private and public reading of Scripture.

The enduring legacy of the Book of Common Prayer is that it is scripturally based, doctrinally sound, and throughly gospel-centered. Dr. John Sentamu, Archbishop of York reminds us, "The Prayer Book places the Bible at the heart of the Church's worship and on the lips of the people. It teaches the grace and mercy of God, and it preaches Jesus as a living Saviour, not a dead master of a by gone age." Its words and prayers are saturated with biblical references and doctrinal themes; it contains the entire book of Psalms; and it has a reading plan to read the entire Bible through regularly. As previously mentioned, J.I. Packer said, "None of us will ever find a better pattern for private prayer and Bible-reading anywhere than that offered by the Prayer Book's own daily offices."

Daily Lectionary

The Book of Common Prayer contains a systematic Bible reading plan called a "Lectionary." A lectionary is simply a list of Bible passages for personal reading and study or for preaching in services of worship. The Lectionary readings from the Book of Common Prayer are used for daily services of worship and for morning and evening prayers. In Cranmer's First Prayer Book of 1549, the lectionary appeared as a lectionary for twelve months, January to December, and provided Old Testament and New Testament lessons for every day of the year. Cranmer intended the Scriptures to be read in morning and evening prayer so that they would become ingrained into the daily rhythms of peoples' lives.

Since that time, there have been many versions of the daily lectionary. Some lectionaries go through the Bible in a year, while other are on a two or three year cycle.

Many of the most recent lectionaries are designed for Sunday services of worship and are organized around the Church Calendar. In recent years, there has been a move towards uniformity among the various lectionaries, such as the Revised Common Lectionary. While many of these lectionaries may help churches follow the Christian Calendar on Sundays, they may not be as helpful for individuals trying to read through the Scriptures in a systematic way. I think Cranmer would agree that reading the entire Bible through in a year is a better approach for individual Christians in private devotion. Regardless of what lectionary or Bible reading plan you follow, there is nothing more important than a regular reading of the Scriptures.

The Original Prayer Book: The Psalms

One of the best ways to begin reading Scripture daily is by starting with the book of Psalms, which is also known as the Psalter. There are exactly 150 Psalms, which expound and explore a wide range of diverse subject matter. Topics such as war, peace, repentance, forgiveness, joy, happiness, worship, praise, and prayer can be found within the pages of the Psalms. The Psalms have provided comfort and guidance for thousands of weary pilgrims who share in the journey of life. The Psalms remind us that we are not alone in our pilgrimage, but that God is with us.

The Psalms have been the prayerbook for God's people since before the time of Christ. Author Eugene Peterson said, "The Psalms were the prayerbook of Israel; they were the prayer book of Jesus; they are the prayer book of the church." They have been a part of the daily rhythm of the church's Bible reading since its earliest days, and they continue to be an important part of the church's private and corporate prayer. It could be said that the reason for the popularity of the Psalms is because they explore a wide range of human emotions and experiences: from delight to despair. In a way, the Psalms express feelings common to all people.

Thomas Cranmer had a profound love and admiration for the Psalms. In fact, he instituted a 30-day cycle of reading the Psalms, which is still printed in the Psalter of the Book of Common Prayer. By following his cycle of daily Psalm readings, you can read through all 150 Psalms on a monthly basis, repeating them twelve times a year. After a while, you will become intimately acquainted with the Psalms in such a powerful way that they will always be with you no matter where you are or what you are going through.

Here is a 30-day cycle for reading through the book of Psalms. In the months which are shorter than thirty days, you can read extra Psalms on the last few days of the month. Likewise, in months with 31 days, you can simply choose additional Psalms readings. Once you have finished the 30-day cycle, you can simply start the journey through the Psalms again on the first day of the next month.

The Lord will meet with you as you prayerfully read through the book of Psalms each month. Cranmer poetically said, "In the scriptures be the fat pastures of the soul." This means that the Scriptures are the very place where we encounter the Lord and where He feeds us with His daily bread. In the spirit of Cranmer, I pray that you would hear, read, mark, learn, and inwardly digest the Scriptures.

30-Day Cycle of Reading the Psalter

Day	Morning	Evening
1	1 - 5	6 - 8
2	9 - 11	12 - 14
3	15 - 17	18
4	19 - 21	22 - 23
5	24 - 26	27 - 29
6	30 - 31	32 - 34
7	35 - 36	37
8	38 - 40	41 - 43
9	44 - 46	47 - 49
10	50 - 52	53 - 55
11	56 - 58	59 - 61
12	62 - 64	65 - 67
13	68	69 - 70
14	71 - 72	73 - 74

15	75 - 77	78
16	79 - 81	82 - 85
17	86 - 88	89
18	90 - 92	93 - 94
19	95 - 97	98 - 101
20	102 - 103	104
21	105	106
22	107	108 - 109
23	110 - 113	114 - 115
24	116 - 118	119:1 - 32
25	119: 33 - 72	119:73 - 104
26	119:105 - 144	119:145 - 176
27	120 - 125	126 - 131
28	132 - 135	136 - 138
29	139 - 140	141 - 143
30	144 - 146	147 - 150

CONCLUSION
Where the Past, Present,
and Future Come Together

"While we need the past, we must not let ourselves become imprisoned by it or allow it to become an idol." -Esther de Waal

This is not just a prayer book about reliving the past. On the contrary, the purpose of *Our Common Prayer* is to show how the past, present, and future can come together through prayer. The church of the past can speak to the present, and the church of the present can reach into the future with a faith that is rooted and grounded in Christ in a dynamic way. Author and Bishop Todd Hunter describes it in the following way:

> "The Book of Common Prayer is going missional! Leading us by prayer into a kingdom and missional worldview, I see the Book of Common Prayer shaping the community of Jesus one life at a time, as we become his cooperative friends, living in creative goodness, through the power of the Holy Spirit, for the sake of others."

Some Christians may think that common prayer does not allow room for freedom of the Spirit. Nothing could be further from the truth. In the preface of the Book of Common Prayer it says, "It is a most invaluable part of that blessed liberty wherewith Christ hath made us free, that in his worship, different forms and usages may without offense be allowed, provided the substance of the Faith be kept entire."

Common prayer provides us with a structure for our prayer, not a straight jacket that binds us. Common prayer gives us a foundation, which on one hand keeps us grounded and on the other frees us to be open to the leading of the Holy Spirit.

A growing number of Christians from various backgrounds are beginning to open up the treasure chest of church history to find ancient tools and practices to live out the faith in the postmodern world. That is not to say that common prayer is the only way that Christians should pray, neither is it for everybody. However, common prayer has been a tool that has enriched the faith of millions of Christians around the world for hundreds of years and still has the power to offer a vibrant, healthy, life-giving faith for our generation and generations to come.

I have found in the historic common prayer tradition an oasis in the desert, a river in dry and thirsty land, and a treasure hidden among the clamor of our postmodern society. It is a great gift that I want to share with the world. It has changed my life, and I want to encourage others to discover this beautiful tradition for themselves. God's gifts are meant to be shared in common. If God has inspired and encouraged you through these prayers, then pass it on and share the gift of common prayer with others.

BOOK OF COMMON PRAYER TIMELINE

1549: Act of Uniformity; first Book of Common Prayer; 'Prayer Book' rebellion

1552: Second, revised Book of Common Prayer

1553: Death of Edward VI; accession of Mary I

1554: Reunion with Rome; Act abolishing Book of Common Prayer

1556: Cranmer burned at the stake

1558: Accession of Queen Elizabeth I

1559: Act of Uniformity; third Book of Common Prayer

1603: Accession of James VI of Scotland as James I

1604: Hampton Court Conference; fourth Book of Common Prayer

1625: Accession of Charles I

1637: Scottish Book of Common Prayer; causes unrest

1642: Civil War begins

1645: Book of Common Prayer abolished by Parliament

1649: Trial and execution of Charles I

1653: Oliver Cromwell becomes Lord Protector

1658: Death of Oliver Cromwell, the protectorate passes to his son Richard

1660: Restoration of Charles II; review of Book of Common Prayer proposed by Earl of Clarendon, Lord Chancellor

1661: Savoy Conference to revise Book of Common Prayer

1662: Act of Uniformity; revised Book of Common Prayer

PRAISE FOR THE BOOK OF COMMON PRAYER

"I believe there is no Liturgy in the world, either in ancient or modern language, which breathes more of a solid, scriptural, rational piety than the Common Prayer of the Church of England."
-John Wesley

"The Bible first, the Prayer Book next, and all other books and doings in subordination to both."
-Charles Simeon

"It is probably true to say that there is no book in existence, apart from the Bible, which is so well known and yet so little appreciated, as the Book of Common Prayer. Every Sunday a very large number of people throughout the world, hold it and use it, and yet probably very few have ever really considered what an immense value there is in a liturgical form of worship."
-J.C. Ryle

"At its greatest it shines with a white light hardly surpassed outside the pages of the New Testament itself."
-C.S. Lewis on the Book of Common Prayer

"Years ago when I wanted to become more skillful in public prayer, I was fortunate to come across the collects of Thomas Cranmer, the writer of the original Episcopal Book of Common Prayer."
-Tim Keller

"I love the weekly Collects in the Book of Common Prayer... Again and again they outshine, in their elegant but profound synthesis, more recent attempts to capture Christian truth and turn it into prayer."
-N.T. Wright

"Long before the age of fish and chips, the Book of Common Prayer was the great British invention, nurturing all sorts and conditions of Englishmen and holding the church together with remarkable effectiveness."
-J.I. Packer

"I consider The Book of Common Prayer, which after the Bible forms the worship and spiritual formation of Anglicans, to be one of God's great gifts to the church."
-Scot McKnight

"There is a fitting sense of awe before God in the Prayer Book, and awe is one of the things which is most notably lacking in contemporary Christianity."
-Dr. Michael Green

"As somebody who was brought up on that prayer book- day after day, year after year, Sunday after Sunday, school worship after school worship, evening prayer, communion, everything- those words do sink into your soul in some extraordinary way."
-Prince Charles of Whales

"The words of the Book of Common Prayer have a rare capacity not only to sink into the memory through their rhythms but to calm the very pace of our thoughts. They are words that help us to be open and still, to recognise with sober humility the greatness of what confronts us in the mysteries of our redemption."
-Archbishop of Canterbury Rowan Williams

"The Prayer Book places the Bible at the heart of the Church's worship and on the lips of the people. It teaches the grace and mercy of God, and it preaches Jesus as a living Saviour, not a dead master of a bygone age. The presence and power of the Holy Spirit is constantly acknowledged."
-Archbishop of York Dr. John Sentamu

"The Book of Common Prayer which immerses us in the whole symphony of scripture; which takes us through the Psalms every month; which makes available in a digestible but noble way the treasury of ancient Christian devotion has a beauty which is ancient but also fresh."
-Dr. Richard Chartres, Bishop of London

"The Book of Common Prayer has endured, still endures and will endure in the minds of men because it is full of truth, and perhaps above all because of its honesty about man's weakness and inability to stand upright without the aid of divine grace."
-Peter Hitchens, Author

"The Book of Common Prayer is one of the great treasuries of the English language. The cadences and poetry of its language were a profound influence on me and on the way in which I write. I owe that marvellous book so much."
-Professor Alexander McCall Smith

SUGGESTIONS FOR FUTHER READING

The Book of Common Prayer, New York: Church Publishing, 1979.

Benson, Robert. *Constant Prayer.* Nashville: Thomas Nelson, 2009.

Black, Vicki K. *Welcome to the Book of Common Prayer.* Morehouse Publishing. Harrisburg, PA. 2005.

Bradshaw, Paul F. *Daily Prayer in the Early Church: A Study of the Origin and Early Development of the Divine Office.* Eugene, OR: Wipf & Stock Publishers, 2008.

Cary, George. *Celebrating Common Prayer.* New York: Continuum, 1999.

Chittster, Joan. *The Liturgical Year.* Nashville: Thomas Nelson, 2009.

Community of Jesus. *The Little Book of Hours: Praying with the Community of Jesus.* Brewster, Massachusetts: Paraclete Press, 2007.

Galli, Mark. *Beyond Smells and Bells: The Wonder and Power of Christian Liturgy.* Brewster, MA. Paraclete Press. 2008.

Hatchett, Marion J. *Commentary on the American Prayer Book.* New York: The Seabury Press, 1981.

Jeffrey, Lee. *Opening the Prayer Book, The New Church's Teaching Series*, Vol 7. Cambridge, MA: Crowley Publications, 1999.

MacCulloch, Diarmaid. *Thomas Cranmer. A Life*. New Haven: Yale University Press, 1996.

Marshall, Paul V. *Prayer Book Parallels: The Public Services of the Church Arranged for Comparative Study*. New York: The Church Hymnal Corporation, 1989.

Merton, Thomas. *A Book of Hours*. Notre Dame, IN: Sorin Books, 2007.

McKnight, Scot. *Praying with the Church: Following Jesus, Daily, Hourly, Today*. Brewster, Massachusetts: Paraclete Press, 2006.

Morgan, Dewi. *1662 and All That: Commemorating the Third Centenary of the Book of Common Prayer*. London: A.R. Mowbray & Co., Limited & Co., Limited, 1961.

Saint Benedict's *Prayer Book for Beginners*. Ampleforth Abbey, York, UK: Ampleforth Abbey Press, 1994.

Sydnor, William. *The Study of the Real Prayer Book: 1549 to the Present*. Wilton, CT: Morehouse Publishing, 1978.

The Northumbria Community. *Celtic Daily Prayer: Prayers and Readings From the Northumbria Community.* New York: HarperOne, 2002.

Tickle, Phyllis. *The Divine Hours: Prayers for Summertime,* New York: Doubleday Books. 2000.

_____. *The Divine Hours: Prayers for Autom and Winter,* New York: Doubleday Books. 2000.

_____. *The Divine Hours: Prayers for Springtime,* New York: Doubleday Books. 2000.

Wainwright, Geoffrey & Karen B. Westerfield Tucker, eds. *The Oxford History of Christian Worship.* Oxford / New York: Oxford University Press, 2006.

Westerhoff, John H. *Living Faithfully as a Prayer Book People.* Harisburg: Morehouse Publishing, 2004.

ABOUT THE AUTHOR

Winfield Bevins is founding pastor of Church of the Outer Banks and Canon for Church Planting for the Diocese of the Carolinas. He is the author of several books, including *Creed: Connect to the Basic Essentials of Historic Christian Faith*. He speaks at conferences, workshops, and retreats throughout the United States on a variety of topics. He has a Doctorate from Southeastern Seminary in Wake Forest, North Carolina.

Winfield lives in the beautiful beach community of the Outer Banks of North Carolina with his wife Kay and three daughters Elizabeth, Anna Belle, and Caroline. He loves to surf, paint, and take long walks on the beach with his family. On any given day, he can be found at the local coffee shop reading a book or talking with others about life and faith.

Discover more Online

www.ourcommonprayer.com

www.creedthebook.com

Made in United States
Orlando, FL
25 April 2023

32470842R00093